Vulnerable Inside

CHILDREN IN SECURE AND PENAL SETTINGS

Barry Goldson

The
Children's
Society

First published in 2002

The Children's Society
Edward Rudolf House
Margery Street
London WC1X 0JL

A catalogue record of this book is available from the British Library.

ISBN 1 899783 43 1

Contents

Tables

Acknowledgements

Writing this book has been a privilege. In undertaking the research that lies at its core, I met a wide range of fine people who took the time to share their knowledge, insight and experiences with me. Moreover, many of the same people took me into their confidence and I am privileged to have been so entrusted.

However, completing the research and writing the book has also been painful. Entering locked institutions where children are held is no fun. Observing the sadness which children normally exude in such places is distressing. Interviewing them, and listening to their stories, can often be uplifting in respect of their youthful energy, keen humour, insight and resilience, but it can also be a profoundly depressing experience. At times, after lengthy interviewing sessions, I left Young Offender Institutions and Secure Units in various parts of England in an emotional daze, a daze which remained with me long after the last interview. In helping me to make sense of such feelings I am indebted to Alison Liebling, for in the midst of undertaking my interviews I read her excellent paper *Doing Research in Prison: Breaking the Silence?* Alison's paper also served to restore my confidence in the legitimacy of my primary methods. She asks, 'So, am I a criminologist?', before answering, 'Yes, I am also a human being, and any methodological approach which asks for separation between these two features of our lives or work is deeply flawed' (Liebling, 1999: 166). The same can probably be said of any social research within locked institutions. So, it was because the methodological approach was not 'flawed' that, as a 'human being',

I was so moved by what I found. It could hardly be otherwise. Two particular incidents have left indelible impressions.

The first, arriving early one Saturday morning at a Young Offender Institution, I was soon to learn that a 16-year-old boy had been found hanging the previous evening. When I arrived the child – who had been moved to the local hospital – was clinging to life with the help of an artificial respirator. By mid-day he was dead. If ever it can be 'just another prison suicide', it is far more than that when you come so close.

The second, sharing sandwiches and lunchtime banter with a group of children and staff in a Secure Unit while, unbeknown to us, another child, a young girl alone in her bedroom, was cutting away at her wrists. Again, at such proximity, this was more than a standard 'self-harm statistic'.

These incidents are extreme expressions of children's distress in locked institutions. They are located at the most harrowing end of the vulnerability continuum. However, there are many other more 'routine' points on that same continuum, and, taken together, they pose discomforting questions for policy and practice with regard to such children. I hope that this book may contribute to the stock of such questions.

Completing the research for this book would not have been possible without the direct commission from The Children's Society, and a generous contribution to the research funds from the Youth Justice Board for England and Wales. I am obliged to both. Furthermore, I am grateful to the senior personnel from the four Young Offender Institutions and six Secure Units, who granted me access and provided me with the necessary permissions to undertake interviews. For purposes of confidentiality however, I am unable to name either the staff or the establishments. Nor can I name any of the 111 individuals who I interviewed during the course of the research, but my thanks go to each and every one of them. I am especially grateful to the children who participated in the research process and I have tried to write to each of them to express such gratitude. I would like to reiterate my thanks and best wishes to them all again.

In addition to the people who agreed to be formally interviewed, I also consulted with many others to whom I am indebted including colleagues from the Department of Health, the Home Office, the Howard League for Penal Reform, Inquest, Nacro, the National Association for Youth Justice, Secure Accommodation Network, and the Youth Justice Board for England and Wales. Furthermore, I would like to thank the particular member of staff from one of the participating Young Offender Institutions who provided crucial help with auditing various forms of assessment data; to everyone who completed the Secure Accommodation questionnaire; and to the library staff at The Children's Society, the National Children's Bureau and The University of Liverpool.

The research process has been very time-consuming and I would like to thank various colleagues from the Department of Sociology, Social Policy and Social Work Studies at The University of Liverpool, not only for bearing with me during this time, but also for listening and for providing advice, support and encouragement at crucial moments. For this, I am particularly grateful to Janet Jamieson and to Chris Jones. Further support and encouragement, together with considerable patience and understanding as various 'deadlines' passed, came from the Vulnerability Research Reference Group, and I wish to record my thanks to the core members of that group: David Asher, Justine Ashton, Henny Heawood and Eleanor Peters.

Finally, my appreciation goes to each of the people who have read and commented upon earlier draft versions of the book, and to Juliette Bright, Madeleine Metcalfe and Caroline Pook for their technical support throughout the production process.

I offer this book to all those who aim to make a positive difference for vulnerable children. Thank you too.

BARRY GOLDSON
June 2002

CHAPTER *1*

Researching children's vulnerability in secure and penal settings

INTRODUCTION

This book is the product of an intensive 12-month research project that has aimed both to investigate the vulnerabilities of children held in secure and penal settings, and to analyse the practices used to assess and address such vulnerabilities. The primary research focus relates to two discrete groups of children, or to be more precise, to two distinct legal routes along which children are processed into specific types of locked institution. Children who are placed in *secure accommodation* under *civil/welfare statute*, and those who are held in *Young Offender Institutions* under *criminal justice/remand legislation*, are the core concern of the book and herein lies a certain paradox.

The vulnerabilities of children placed in secure accommodation under the provisions of civil/welfare law are considered to be so great in the community, that institutional confinement is sanctioned by the courts in order to keep them safe. Here the restriction of the child's liberty is regarded as a necessary and benign means to safeguard and promote their welfare. Not surprisingly, however, the practice of locking up children in order to serve their 'best interests' and the concept of 'incarcerative child-care' (Goldson, 1992) raise certain concerns and these are examined in Chapter 2.

The rationale for remanding children into Young Offender

Institutions is quite different. Here, it is the risk that children are thought to pose *to* the community, rather than the vulnerabilities that they might experience *within* it, that is at stake. Protection of the public takes precedence over protection of the child, and the withdrawal of liberty is legitimised by the imperatives of community safety as distinct from those of child welfare. There are, however, concerns about the treatment and conditions endured by children subject to penal remands; the locked institution, rather than being seen as a place of safety, is regarded as a potential place of danger (Goldson and Peters, 2000; Howard League, 1995 and 1997; Her Majesty's Chief Inspector of Prisons, 1997, 2000 and 2001; Penal Affairs Consortium, 1996). The detail of such concern is discussed in Chapter 3.

The paradox, therefore, is that the locked institution can be seen as *relief from vulnerability* for one identifiable group of children, and as a *source of vulnerability* for another, according to its nature, its particular statutory purpose and its specific operational function. Moreover, the way in which children are formally viewed lies at the root of such paradox. Hendrick (1994) has identified what he calls a 'victim-threat dualism' whereby children can be seen either as troubled and in need of protection (the child as *victim*), or as troublesome and in need of correction and control (the child as *threat*). Furthermore, such perception, at least in part, has a significant bearing upon the nature of professional responses to children who come to the attention of state agencies, and the legal routes along which they are processed (Goldson, 1995; Malek, 1993).

Despite such tidy conceptual differentiation, the children at the core of this research can rarely, if ever, be simply placed in either the 'victim/troubled/vulnerable' or the 'threat/troublesome/risk' pigeon-hole. There is much interaction and overlap within and between such distinct categories, and the backgrounds, social circumstances and experiences of these children are extremely complex and often similar, as discussed in Chapter 7. This book attempts to illuminate such complexity; to explore the vulnerabilities of all such children; to assess critically institutional practices; and to consider the primary issues for policy makers, child welfare and youth justice managers and practitioners, and, perhaps most importantly of all, for the children themselves.

In engaging with such issues, the research has taken place at a time of significant change to secure and penal settings for children. Since April 1 2000, the Youth Justice Board for England and Wales has assumed responsibility for commissioning and purchasing places for all children who are remanded or sentenced to any secure facility within a reconfigured juvenile secure estate (comprising Young Offender Institutions, Local Authority Secure Units and privately managed Secure Training Centres). Although such 'modernising' reform has primarily focused upon improving standards within the youth justice system, its effects have been felt further afield within the child welfare system. The general scope of such reform, and its broad consequences for each of the 'constituencies' of children with whom this book is concerned, is examined in Chapter 4. The specific vulnerabilities of children placed in secure accommodation under welfare statute, and those held on remand in Young Offender Institutions, are explored in Chapters 5 and 6 respectively.

This book was not conceived in terms of academic abstraction. Rather, it is hoped that reading it will unsettle some fixed ideas and contribute to the improvement of welfare and justice services for particular groups of children who are amongst the most damaged and disadvantaged citizens in society. Chapter 7 draws the principal findings together and puts forward proposals for progressing social justice for, and developing appropriate practices with, such children.

THE CORE RESEARCH QUESTIONS

The research was primarily concerned with two discrete and legally defined 'constituencies' of children:

1. Girls and boys placed in secure accommodation with the authority of the Family Proceedings Court under the provisions of the Children Act 1989 – the 'welfare constituency'.
2. Boys aged 15–16 years, denied bail and remanded into a Young Offender Institution by the Youth Court or the Crown Court under criminal justice statute – the 'justice constituency' (the Courts have no powers to remand girls aged 15–16 years into Young Offender Institutions).

The core research questions, which apply to each constituency of children, are essentially five-fold and comprise an investigation of:

1. the instruments, methods and criteria used to assess the vulnerability of children and young people entering secure and penal settings
2. the application/non-application of assessment processes, including both the means by which, and the stage at which, a child's vulnerability is addressed/assessed – or not
3. the consistency of interpretation and application of assessment criteria, and analyses of any variation and/or inconsistency (both within each constituency and between constituencies)
4. the placement supply and demand issue, including how institutional capacity and placement availability might affect the assessment of, and responses to, children's perceived vulnerability
5. children's perceptions of their own vulnerability, the vulnerability of others, and their experiences of secure and penal settings.

THE PRIMARY RESEARCH METHODS

In defining a methodological approach for a study of this nature, and in selecting the most appropriate research methods, a fundamental question is inevitably raised: whether to approach the secure and penal institutions with a qualitative or a quantitative intent. Reflecting upon this dilemma in a different but not entirely dissimilar context, Liebling (1999: 148) concluded: 'in the end, some combination of approach is desirable and necessary'; and so it has been here.

The research design has been modelled to allow an exploration of professional views and operational practices alongside children's experiences of secure 'care' and penal remand; this has primarily been achieved by structured in-depth interviews and individual consultations. Equally, the qualitative dimension of the research has been located within a documented context, which has provided evidence mainly through analyses of policy developments, statistical placement trends and the 'system behaviour' of the 'juvenile secure estate'.

Overall, there are six primary methodological elements:

1. IN-DEPTH INDIVIDUAL INTERVIEWS

A total of 111 interviews were conducted. Eighty of the interviewees were drawn directly from the ten participating secure and penal settings in England (four Young Offender Institutions and six Secure Units). Of these, 25 were children (boys) on penal remand; 15 were children (boys and girls) held in secure units under civil/welfare statute; 20 were staff from Young Offender Institutions (including governor-grade prison officers, principal officers, senior officers and basic-grade officers together with health and education staff, and prison chaplains); and 20 were secure accommodation staff (including senior managers, operational managers and residential social workers).

Fifteen interviews were also held with operational managers and practitioners from The Children's Society National Remand Review Initiative (in the North West of England, London, the West Midlands, and Yorkshire and Humberside – for a detailed description of the work of the National Remand Review Initiative *see* Moore and Smith, 2001: 86–104); and 16 interviews were held with Independent Persons and Children's Guardians involved in the placement of children in secure accommodation under civil/welfare statute, and/or with the review of their cases. At the time of the interviews, Children's Guardians were known as Guardians *ad litem* and Reporting Officers (GALRO) – *see* pp. 15–16.

2. ROUTINE OBSERVATIONS

The interviews were conducted over a period of several months. During the visits to the various secure and penal settings – to negotiate access and make practical arrangements for interviews, to undertake the interviews themselves, as well as during the accumulated hours spent between interviews – there was ample opportunity to observe the practices and operations of the different establishments. Such routine observations served to complement and further illuminate the key messages drawn from interview data.

3. PROFESSIONAL CONSULTATIONS

In addition to the in-depth interviews, many consultations were arranged with representatives of key 'stakeholding' agencies. These included consultations with academics; child and adolescent mental health specialists; children's rights agencies; Department of Health personnel; educationalists and teachers; penal reform organisations; social researchers, social workers; Youth Justice Board personnel and Youth Offending Team workers.

4. DOCUMENTARY SOURCES

To put the field-based research into context, relevant documentary sources have been analysed. These were: academic research, particularly in relation to child welfare, residential care and youth justice; a wide range of publications from children's charities, non-governmental organisations and penal reform agencies; legal documentation including statute, guidance, regulations and standards; reports prepared by the Social Services Inspectorate and Her Majesty's Inspectorate of Prisons; and Department of Health and Home Office statistics.

5. NATIONAL QUESTIONNAIRE SURVEY

Thirty Local Authority Secure Units (LASUs) in England and Wales were sent a questionnaire. The results of the returned questionnaires were collated to provide contextual material about the range and nature of the placement resources within the reformed juvenile secure estate.

6. AUDIT OF ASSESSMENT DOCUMENTATION

An audit of all of the documentation for vulnerability assessments on every juvenile remand prisoner admitted to a single Young Offender Institution over a six-month period was collected and analysed.

VULNERABILITY AND ITS ASSESSMENT

Defining vulnerability is extraordinarily complex, as the Law Commission has observed:

> *Vulnerable people are, or course, not an homogeneous group and arriving at a definition of vulnerability which is neither under- nor over-inclusive presents some difficulties. Vulnerability is, in practice, a combination of characteristics of the person concerned and the risks to which he (sic) is exposed by his particular circumstances.*
>
> *(cited in Home Office, 1998: 20)*

Two points raised by the Law Commission are of particular significance here. First is the question of over- and under-inclusivity, which implies that vulnerability is relative, but also, that the definition reached can be tailored to suit a particular gatekeeping purpose – to avoid either too broad or too limited an application. Second is the distinction between what we might call *innate vulnerability* (which is unique to 'the person concerned'), and *structural* or *contextual vulnerability* (the 'particular circumstances' within which the individual is situated).

The relative nature of vulnerability is immediately apparent if we compare the forms of assessment criteria that apply to children placed in secure accommodation under civil/welfare statute, and those that apply to children remanded to prison service custody (Young Offender Institutions).

For the former group of children the assessments undertaken by social workers and Children's Guardians are informed by official guidance from the Department of Health, and such assessments are likely to be detailed, comprehensive and protracted processes. For example, in fulfilling their statutory duty to safeguard and promote the child's welfare as provided by the Children Act 1989, professionals responsible for assessing such children are required to take account of the 'assessment framework' with detailed consideration of the child's 'developmental needs'; the 'parenting capacities' of those who have parental responsibility for the child; and the 'family and environmental factors' that define the material circumstances within which the child lives (Department of Health, 2000). It is by taking detailed account of all of this (a process which may take several weeks), together with the immediate specifics of the child's behaviour and conduct, that a considered professional judgement will be reached on the vulnerabilities of the child.

However, for the latter group of children (those remanded to penal custody), the time available for a member of a Youth Offending Team and/or a Prison Officer to undertake a vulnerability assessment is exceptionally limited – often no more than a few minutes. Moreover, the fundamental purpose of such an assessment is crudely instrumental: it boils down to making a judgement as to whether the child is likely to harm her/himself or attempt to commit suicide, if they are placed in prison custody. In other words, the time available, the criteria used and the primary purpose of the assessment are fundamentally different for each constituency of child.

An associated issue is the availability of placements within secure accommodation. Whatever the result of a vulnerability assessment of a child from either the welfare or the justice constituency, it is ultimately the availability of secure accommodation that determines whether or not they are left to struggle with their vulnerabilities within the community (for the welfare constituency), and whether or not they are relieved from the pressures of penal custody (for the justice constituency). In other words, irrespective of the outcomes of professional assessment and the child's perceived level of vulnerability, the availability or otherwise of an appropriate placement within secure accommodation will inevitably have the greatest influence in determining the child's fortunes.

The final point to be made here is the relation between 'innate' and 'structural' vulnerability. Every child interviewed during the course of this research could be described as structurally vulnerable (*see* pp. 153–154). Moreover, there are remarkable similarities within the overall sample of children, irrespective of their legally defined status. In this sense the different assessment processes that apply to such children reveal far more about resource exigencies and the different legal pathways along which they are processed, than they do about the vulnerabilities of the children themselves.

These issues, their implications for children, and the means by which they are expressed in practice will be considered in much greater detail in the following chapters.

A NOTE ON 'CHILD' AND 'CHILDREN'

In this book the terms 'child' and 'children' will be taken to apply to 'every human being below the age of eighteen years' in accordance with Article 1 of the United Nations Convention on the Rights of the Child (United Nations General Assembly, 1989), and Section 105 (1) of the Children Act 1989.

CHAPTER *2*

Children in secure accommodation: welfare law, policy and practice

SECURE ACCOMMODATION: ITS DEVELOPMENT AND EXPANSION

According to Dennington (1991: 90) secure accommodation 'has traditionally occupied a unique and ambivalent midpoint on the treatment-punishment continuum'. Other commentators have similarly argued that it is sandwiched 'between hospital and prison or thereabouts' (Harris and Timms, 1993). Secure accommodation straddles the conceptual space that awkwardly separates the child welfare and youth justice systems: it has a foot in both camps. Section 25(1) of the Children Act 1989 defines secure accommodation as 'accommodation provided for the purpose of restricting liberty' and although children can only be placed in such accommodation in strictly defined circumstances, secure units draw their statutory authority from both the civil and the criminal jurisdictions. Consequently, secure units serve to restrict the liberty of a 'comprehensively wide range of children, including suicidal children, drug abusers, child prostitutes, runaways, petty offenders, dangerous and violent children, children on remand and those who have committed extremely serious offences' (Hodgkin, 1995: 4).

The ambiguous status of secure accommodation, the diverse range of children held in secure units and the different 'legal routes' along which they might enter such units (Goldson, 1995; Gabbidon and Goldson, 1997) is a source of both complexity and some controversy. Nevertheless, two discrete waves of development have been discernible in recent years that have enabled secure accommodation to expand and consolidate its position within both the child welfare and youth justice systems.

First, throughout the 1970s and into the 1980s, substantial government grants to local authorities facilitated a considerable expansion of secure provision. Set within a context in which the received wisdom suggested that the public care system – and especially children's homes and other residential provision – was struggling to meet the needs of, and cope with, particularly 'difficult' children and young people, secure units flourished. The central argument was that additional specialised and controlled provision was necessary to contain the more challenging children, so that meaningful work could be undertaken with them in a way that was not considered possible within the mainstream child-care system (Goldson, 1992). However, a number of leading commentators raised serious concerns about the expansion of secure accommodation and the developing rationale that legitimised it. Millham *et al.* (1978) for example, argued that, more than anything, secure units offered relief to the wider system of residential child-care as distinct from explicitly addressing the needs of the children who were contained within them. Others, including Cawson and Martell (1979), drew attention to the element of self-fulfilling prophecy that characterised the expansion of what they called 'closed units':

> . . . *closed provision was justified in terms of its use: the fact that children were being referred and admitted showed that there was a continuing need for children to be placed in closed conditions. The dangers of this process are evident. It provides a formula for the justification of a service regardless of any necessity to demonstrate its value or effectiveness.*
>
> *(cited in Dennington, 1991: 75)*

Or, to put it another way, such practices served to 'generate demand rather than to meet demand' (Cawson and Martell, 1979: 145). The principal problem was that the availability of financial resources that allowed for the expansion of secure accommodation also produced an influx of children into 'closed provision' under questionable circumstances. As one official from the Department of Health was later to observe:

Not surprisingly, many local authorities embraced this largesse with open arms and the late 70s and early 80s saw a rapid expansion of the stock of secure accommodation. Unfortunately, the additional places were rapidly filled with children in local authority care, who, overnight it seemed, suddenly became too difficult to manage in open conditions. You will not be surprised that we are still, even in 1992 . . . wondering how it is possible to provide secure accommodation without it being filled with children who do not really need to be there. (cited in Hodgkin, 1995: 46)

Second, and more recent, has been the expansion of secure accommodation precipitated by developments in youth justice policy in the early 1990s. The abolition of penal remands for children that was anticipated as a result of Section 60 of the Criminal Justice Act 1991 imposed a greater demand for secure accommodation, and such demand was provided for, even though Section 60 was never implemented (*see* pp. 37–40). Similarly, the new arrangements for the remand of 12- to 14-year-old children with 'security requirements', and the amended (and expanded) sentencing criteria of children convicted under Section 53(2) of the Children and Young Persons Act 1933 (both of which were introduced by provisions of the Criminal Justice and Public Order Act 1994), also demanded additional secure accommodation (Goldson, 1995: 2). Indeed, at 31 March 1994, the number of places in secure accommodation in England stood at 282 and the Department of Health calculated that an additional 170 places would be required to meet the increased demand generated by such legislative reform (*ibid*: 3). Accordingly, by 1995 the Secure Accommodation Building Programme set about providing a 60 per cent expansion of closed provision.

More recently still, developments in youth justice law, policy and practice have made a significant impact upon secure accommodation. The Crime and Disorder Act 1998 (which provided for the Detention and Training Order) and the Powers of Criminal Courts (Sentencing) Act 2000 (which amended Section 53 of the Children and Young

Persons Act 1933) have each had tangible effects on secure units. Moreover, such units are subject to further reform within the wider context of the modernisation of the juvenile secure estate, examined in Chapter 4.

Despite the contested (and even controversial) nature of secure accommodation, together with the range of associated concerns that have been raised by researchers over the last 25 years (Cawson and Martell, 1979; Children's Legal Centre, 1982; Goldson, 1995; Harris and Timms, 1993; Hodgkin, 1995; Malek, 1993; Millham *et al.*, 1978; O'Neill, 2001), the stock of secure provision has continued to develop and expand both within the child welfare and youth justice systems. However, it is secure accommodation within the child welfare system that is of primary interest here, and its legal framework and contemporary application are now examined before returning to a more detailed consideration of ongoing concerns.

THE WELFARE ROUTE INTO SECURE ACCOMMODATION: THE LEGAL FRAMEWORK

The purpose of the statutory framework governing the restriction of liberty of children being looked after by local authorities or accommodated by other agencies, is to protect them from unnecessary and inappropriate placement in secure accommodation; to ensure that administrative decisions taken by the local authority or others within that framework are scrutinised and endorsed by the court, and to ensure that any such placements are only for as long as is necessary and appropriate.

(Department of Health, 1993: para 8.9)

SECTION 25 – CHILDREN ACT 1989

For a child being 'looked after' by a local authority, either because they are subject to a Care Order (as provided by Section 31 of the Children Act 1989) or because they are accommodated by voluntary agreement (as provided by Section 20 of the same Act), the criteria for admission to secure accommodation are set out in Section 25 of the Children Act 1989:

(a) (i) he (sic) has a history of absconding and is likely to abscond from any other description of accommodation; and

(ii) if he absconds, he is likely to suffer significant harm; or

(b) that if he is kept in any other description of accommodation he is likely to injure himself or other persons.

The local authority initially has primary responsibility for determining whether these criteria are met and whether a placement in a secure unit is necessary. Where such placements are to exceed 72 hours (or 72 hours aggregated in any period over 28 days), the local authority must refer the case to a Family Proceedings Court (Department of Health, 1991: Regulation 10). The maximum periods that a court may authorise for a child to be kept in secure accommodation are three months on the first application (Department of Health, 1991: Regulation 11), or six months for any further application from the local authority (Department of Health, 1991: Regulation 12). No child under the age of 13 may be placed in secure accommodation via the welfare route without the prior approval of the Secretary of State (Department of Health, 1991: Regulation 4).

A number of the concerns (relating to locking up children within the child welfare system) signalled at the beginning of this chapter (*see* pp. 9–10), and discussed in more detail later (*see* pp. 23–24), are apparently recognised and endorsed by the official guidance that has been issued by the Department of Health:

Restricting the liberty of children is a serious step which must be taken only when there is no appropriate alternative. It must be a 'last resort' in the sense that all else must first have been comprehensively considered and rejected – never because no other placement was available at the relevant time, because of inadequacies in staffing, because the child is simply being a nuisance or runs away from his (sic) accommodation and is not likely to cause significant harm in doing so, and never as a form of punishment. It is important, in considering the possibility of secure placement, that there is a clear view of the aims and objectives of such a placement and that those providing the accommodation can fully meet those aims and objectives. Secure placements, once made, should be only for so long as is necessary and unavoidable.

(Department of Health, 1993: para 8.5)

In making an application for a Secure Accommodation Order under the provisions of Section 25 of the Children Act 1989, such guidance requires the local authority and the court to be convinced that:

1. such restriction of liberty is the *only way* – after all else has been comprehensively considered and rejected – of responding to the likelihood of a child suffering significant harm or causing injury to herself/himself or to others

2. the aims and objectives of the secure 'placement' are clearly set out and the secure unit staff are capable of meeting them

3. the placement is an integral part of a care plan for the child, which includes an explicitly defined strategy for continuity of care once the placement ends

4. so far as is reasonably practicable full account has been taken of the wishes and feelings of the child, her/his parents, any other person with parental responsibility, and any other person whose wishes and feelings may be considered relevant

5. paramount consideration has been given to the child's welfare.

(*see* Department of Health, 1993: paras 8.5, 8.7, 8.9).

THE COURT

Any application to place a child in secure accommodation via the welfare route must be made to a Family Proceedings Court.

THE CHILD

The child need not be present when the local authority applies for a Secure Accommodation Order. It has been suggested that the court should only allow the child to attend if it is satisfied that it would be in her/his interests (Ashford and Chard, 2000: 297).

LEGAL REPRESENTATION

Section 25(6) of the Children Act 1989 provides that no Family Proceedings Court is able to authorise the placement of a child in secure accommodation who has not been legally represented unless, having been informed of the right to legal representation, the child has declined her/his right. There is a presumption that the child will be legally represented and the official guidance states that:

*... children should be encouraged to appoint a legal representative
... and given every assistance to make such arrangements ... The
child in such circumstances should have details of local solicitors on
the Law Society's Child Care Panel made available to him (sic) and
should be assisted in making contact with the solicitor of his choice.*

(Department of Health, 1993: para 8.40)

THE GUARDIAN AD LITEM (THE CHILDREN'S GUARDIAN)

*Because restricting a child's liberty is such a serious matter
proceedings under section 25 have been specified under the Rules
of Court as requiring the appointment of a guardian ad litem except
where the court does not consider this is necessary to protect the
welfare of the child. (Department of Health, 1993: para 8.9).*

Until April 2001, local authorities were required by law to provide
panels of Guardians *ad litem* who are independent of them, and from
which the Family Proceedings Courts are able to make appointments.
Timms (1995) has argued that representing children in secure
accommodation proceedings under the provisions of Section 25 of
the Children Act 1989 is one of the most important areas of work for
the Guardian *ad litem*.

However, the Criminal Justice and Court Services Act 2000
established the Children and Family Court Advisory Support Service
(CAFCASS), a non-departmental public body accountable to the
Lord Chancellor's Department. In turn, CAFCASS has consolidated
the services that furnish the courts with expert opinion in relation to
the welfare of children and their families. Before CAFCASS, such
advice was provided by the Family Court Welfare Service, the
Guardian *ad litem* and Reporting Officer (GALRO) service, and the
Children's Divisions of the Official Solicitor's Department.
CAFCASS has thus streamlined such arrangements and, from April
2001, Guardians *ad litem* have become known as Children's
Guardians. Despite the change of name, they retain the same
functions in respect of secure accommodation.

As soon as possible after the start of secure accommodation
proceedings, the Clerk to the Court should normally appoint a
Children's Guardian and, once appointed, the child's solicitor is

required to act on their instructions. The primary duties of the Children's Guardian are to safeguard the interests of the child; to ensure that the child has an effective voice in court by representing her/his 'ascertainable wishes and feelings'; to seek to avoid delays in the case being heard and/or determined; and to have regard to the 'welfare checklist' as provided by Section 1 of the Children Act 1989. Additionally the Guardian is required to advise the Family Proceedings Court on the child's level of understanding; the child's wishes; the suitability of the options available to the court; and on any other matter on which the Guardian's advice is sought (for a more detailed discussion *see* McCausland, 2000).

SECURE ACCOMMODATION REVIEWS

A specific reviewing process (separate from, and additional to, the system of statutory reviews that apply to all 'looked after' children as provided by Section 26 of the Children Act 1989) is required for children placed in secure accommodation via the welfare route. Regulation 15 of the relevant Statutory Instrument provides that every child placed in a secure unit should have her/his case reviewed 'within one month of the inception of the placement and then at intervals not exceeding three months where the child continues to be kept in such accommodation' (Department of Health, 1991). Moreover, for the purposes of conducting each review, local authorities are required to appoint at least three people, one of whom should not be employed by the local authority looking after the child or by the local authority managing the secure unit in which the child is held (the 'Independent Person').

Regulation 16(1) (Department of Health, 1991) requires those appointed to conduct the review to consider whether or not:

(a) the criteria for keeping the child in secure accommodation . . .
   continue to apply, and
(b) such a placement continues to be necessary and whether or not
   any other description of accommodation would be appropriate
   for (the child);
and in so doing they must have regard for the welfare of the child.
                                        (Department of Health, 1993: para 8.54)

Furthermore, regulations 16(2) and 16(3) (Department of Health, 1991) require those appointed to undertake the review to ascertain, and to take into account, as far as is practicable, the wishes and feelings of:

(a) *the child,*

(b) *any parent of his (sic),*

(c) *any person not being a parent of his but who has parental responsibility for him,*

(d) *any other person who has had the care of the child, whose views the persons appointed consider should be taken into account,*

(e) *the child's independent visitor if one has been appointed, and*

(f) *the local authority managing the secure accommodation in which the child is placed if that authority is not the authority looking after the child. (Department of Health, 1993: para 8.55)*

On the face of it therefore, the reviewing process provides a safeguard against any possibility of a child having their liberty restricted within the child welfare system for any longer than is absolutely necessary. However, there are concerns relating to this issue, the first of which is indicated in the official guidance itself, which states:

If a conclusion of the reviewing panel is that the criteria for restricting liberty no longer apply, the placement is no longer necessary or other accommodation is appropriate, the authority looking after the child must immediately review the child's placement. (Department of Health, 1993: para 8.56)

In other words, if the reviewing panel concludes that it is no longer necessary to hold the child in a secure unit, the placing authority is only obliged 'to immediately review the child's placement' as distinct from immediately removing the child from secure conditions and thus restoring her/his liberty. This issue is considered in more detail below, and in greater detail still in Chapter 5 (*see* pp. 114–119).

THE WELFARE ROUTE INTO SECURE ACCOMMODATION: CHILDREN'S RIGHTS

In addition to the statutory framework that determines the welfare route into secure accommodation (together with its various inherent safeguards), international standards, treaties and rules also have a bearing upon such processes (most notably the United Nations Convention on the Rights of the Child), as does the Human Rights Act 1998.

THE UNITED NATIONS CONVENTION ON THE RIGHTS OF THE CHILD

The UN Convention on the Rights of the Child (United Nations General Assembly, 1989) is the first detailed international treaty to provide comprehensive minimum standards for the treatment of all children. The UK Government ratified the treaty in December 1991, thus committing itself to making the rights in the Convention a reality for all children in the UK (Children's Rights Development Unit, 1994). The application of the UN Convention is particularly relevant to secure accommodation, especially its provisions that aim to confer adequate protection from all forms of ill-treatment and abuse, and from arbitrary and unlawful restriction of liberty. Article 37 states Parties shall ensure that:

> (b) *No child shall be deprived of his or her liberty unlawfully or arbitrarily. The (restriction of liberty) . . . shall be used only as a measure of last resort and for the shortest appropriate period of time.*
>
> (c) *Every child deprived of liberty shall be treated with humanity and respect for the inherent dignity of the human person, and in a manner which takes into account the needs of persons of his or her age. (United Nations General Assembly, 1989)*

Equally many other Articles of the UN Convention can be seen to apply to children placed in secure accommodation via the welfare route including:

- Article 2, which provides for non-discrimination
- Article 3, which provides for the best interests of the child

- Article 9, which limits the circumstances in which a child should be separated from her/his parents
- Article 12, which provides the child's right to have their views taken into account
- Article 16, which provides for the protection of the child's privacy
- Article 19, which provides for the protection of the child from abuse and neglect
- Article 20, which provides for the protection of children without families
- Article 24, which provides for the child's highest attainable standard of health
- Article 25, which provides for periodic reviews of placements
- Article 27, which provides for the child's right to benefit from an adequate standard of living
- Articles 28 and 29, which provide for the child's right to appropriate education
- Article 30, which provides for the rights of children from minority ethnic communities to enjoy their own culture, practice their religion and use their own language
- Article 31, which provides for the child's right to leisure and recreational activities
- Article 33, which provides for the protection of children from drug abuse
- Article 34, which provides for the protection of children from sexual abuse and exploitation.

THE HUMAN RIGHTS ACT 1998

The Human Rights Act, which came into effect in October 2000, has served to incorporate provisions from the European Convention on Human Rights (ECHR) into UK law, and it requires all other legislation to be interpreted and given effect compatibly with the Convention rights. Unlike the UN Convention on the Rights of the Child, the ECHR was not compiled specifically with children in mind. Nevertheless, the European Court's rulings have increasingly acknowledged the special vulnerabilities of children. Indeed, not unlike the UN Convention on the Rights of the Child, many of the provisions of the ECHR can be seen to apply to children placed in secure accommodation via the welfare route including:

* Article 3, which provides for the right to freedom from inhuman and degrading treatment
* Article 5, which provides for the right to liberty and security of person
* Article 6, which provides for the right to a fair trial and which includes civil cases and regulatory procedures
* Article 8, which provides for the right to respect for private and family life
* Article 14, which prohibits discrimination in the enjoyment of Convention rights.

McFarlane (2001: 276) has observed that before the implementation of the Human Rights Act in October 2000 'it was oft said that the regime for making secure accommodation orders under Children Act 1989 s.25, was likely to be an early target for attack . . . on the grounds that the statutory scheme could not be compatible with the European Convention on Human Rights'. Indeed, such a challenge has been made on the basis that Section 25 of the Children Act 1989 was incompatible with Article 5 of the ECHR. While this appears to make perfect sense on the face of it, Dawson and Stephens (1991) have described the complexities integral to the statutory framework that applies to secure accommodation as a 'legal labyrinth'. Also, following a particularly complex ruling, the Court of Appeal concluded that Section 25 was not incompatible with Article 5 (Children's Legal Centre, 2001: 20) thus, according to McFarlane (2001: 277) 'laying to rest the argument'.

CHILDREN IN SECURE ACCOMMODATION: PATTERNS IN THE PRACTICE OF RESTRICTING LIBERTY

The most recent published statistics reveal that on 31 March 2001 there were 450 places available in 30 secure units maintained by local authorities in England and Wales: 432 in England and 18 in Wales (Department of Health, 2001). When the total number of occupied secure places in England is examined over a period of ten years, the figures testify to the patterns of expansion and increasing use that were signalled at the beginning of this chapter. In 1992, therefore, the number of available places in secure units in England stood at 274, and 238 of such places were occupied. Ten years later the corresponding figures are 432 and 377 representing a 58 per cent increase in both the supply and use of secure accommodation.

Table 1: Children in secure accommodation in England 1992–2001 (actual numbers)

At 31 March	1992	1993	1994	1995	1996	1997	1998	1999	2000	2001
Places approved[1]	274	271	289	266	274	328	416	434	436	432
Children placed	238	251	244	233	246	279	333	324	366	377
Occupancy rate (%)	87	93	84	88	90	85	80	75	84	87

Source: Department of Health (2001)

[1] Secure unit places have to be formally approved/licenced by the Department of Health

However, despite such overall expansion, the pattern of use which specifically relates to children placed in secure accommodation via the welfare route has remained more or less constant. Moreover, the most recent figures even suggest a contraction.

Table 2: Children placed via the welfare route in secure accommodation in England 1992–2001 (actual numbers)

At 31 March	1992	1993	1994	1995	1996	1997	1998	1999	2000	2001
Children placed[1]	63	80	89	76	75	74	91	78	79	64

Source: Department of Health (2001)

[1] This includes all looked-after children placed in secure units, that is, those subject to Care Orders and those accommodated by voluntary agreement.

Such patterns of use become particularly interesting with regard to the mix of children being placed in secure units. If the overall supply of secure accommodation has increased by 58 per cent and yet the number of children placed via the welfare route has either remained constant or lessened, it follows that the additional capacity has been filled by children placed via the justice route, which has significant implications for the proportionate mix of children within secure units. Indeed, children placed via the welfare route have traditionally comprised approximately one third of all children in secure accommodation but the most recent figures suggest that they now represent nearer one fifth. In other words, secure accommodation is transforming into a more orthodox youth justice resource, and children whose liberty is restricted under the provisions of welfare statute represent a diminishing minority in proportionate terms.

Table 3: Children placed via the welfare route and justice route in secure accommodation in England 1992–2001

At 31 March	1992	1993	1994	1995	1996	1997	1998	1999	2000	2001
Welfare route[1]	26%	32%	36%	33%	31%	26%	28%	24%	21%	17%
Justice route[2]	74%	68%	64%	67%	69%	74%	72%	76%	79%	83%

Source: Department of Health (2001)

[1] As with Table 2, this includes all looked-after children placed in secure units, that is, those subject to Care Orders and those accommodated by voluntary agreement.
[2] This includes all children placed under the provisions of criminal justice statute, that is, remanded and sentenced children.

The changing patterns in the practice of restricting the liberty of children will be examined in greater detail in Chapters 3 and 4. For now it is simply noted that children whose liberty is restricted under the provisions of welfare statute have a diminishing 'market share' of secure accommodation within the wider context of overall expansion. This raises some concerns about balancing the mix of children within any single secure unit (*see* Chapters 4 and 5).

LOCKED UP IN CARE: SOME CONCERNS ABOUT THE WELFARE ROUTE INTO SECURE ACCOMMODATION

Placing children in secure accommodation via the welfare route epitomises difficult tensions between care and control, and raises many complex issues relating to ethics, human rights and professional licence. Hodgkin, for example, questions:

> . . . why exactly is it necessary to lock up young people who are only a risk to themselves? What if their behaviour is untreatable within the locked placement? . . . Is it legitimate to lock up a child if 'other description of accommodation' (such as open accommodation) **could** be used but is not, for whatever reason, available? . . . How can one determine which to lock up of the many thousands of young people whose behaviours make them eligible for security . . . ? What filters, judicial or otherwise, ensure that **only** the necessary minimum are locked up? (Hodgkin, 1995: 7, original emphasis)

Indeed, many such concerns were raised – by professionals and children alike – in the course of undertaking the research for this book, and these are considered in more detail in Chapter 5. For now however, six of the most pressing issues will be explored.

CONCERN 1: INDIVIDUAL PATHOLOGY OR SYSTEMIC FAILURE?

Various studies have indicated that the calibre of residential social work staff, the resources available to them, and the culture of residential settings for children in the public care system, play a significant role in determining the quality of outcomes for looked-after children (*see*, for example, Gabbidon and Goldson, 1998 and Sinclair and Gibbs, 1998). Indeed, there is little mystery in the relationship between well-managed and adequately resourced child-care systems and positive outcomes, just as the reverse is true, as Bullock and Little have observed:

> Research has shown that much difficult adolescent behaviour is contextual in that it is influenced by the regimes experienced by young people . . . Thus bad institutions are more likely than good ones to produce more candidates for security.
>
> (Bullock and Little, 1991: 2)

In other words, the behaviour of a child is likely to reveal just as much about the quality of her/his care as about the child her/himself (Vernon, 1995). However, there is a tendency to take the challenging behaviours and vulnerabilities of looked-after children out of context, reducing them to the level of individual pathology, as if unconnected to the impact of the wider child-care system. Following a lengthy research study, Aymer and her colleagues noted that:

The assessments we read tended to locate the origins of the problematic situations in which these young people played a central role within the young people themselves rather than in the networks of which they were part. As such they ran the risk of perpetrating what psychologists call the 'fundamental attribution error' in which situations which arise out of interactions between the actor and his or her environment are wrongly perceived as an expression of their intrinsic characteristics. (Aymer et al., 1991: 98)

Thus it is not unreasonable to suggest that the behaviours and vulnerabilities of children may be more effectively addressed by intervening in the failing systems that create them, rather than resorting to the restriction of individual liberty. Indeed, the evidence suggests that some placements in secure accommodation could be avoided by raising the standards of care within 'open' provision and by devising more imaginative alternatives to locking up children (Hodgkin, 1995; O'Neill, 2001).

CONCERN 2: THE PLACEMENT LOTTERY

The above concern is further confirmed by research into the characteristics, behaviours and vulnerabilities of children who have their liberty restricted via the welfare route. Thus O'Neill (1999: 290) observes that 'it seems that many young people in secure accommodation are not significantly different from those accommodated in non-secure provision', and Aymer and her colleagues note that:

. . . it is not necessarily the hard core of dangerous and self-damaging children and young people, those for whom secure accommodation was designed, who go into security . . . but those

who test out an overstretched staff team, fail to conform to institutional rules or just do not 'fit in' anywhere else. This was our finding and it . . . begs questions about who is being locked up and why? (Aymer et al., 1991: 93)

Similar findings have also been reported by Hodgkin (1995), O'Neill (2001) and Vernon (1995). Indeed, despite the ostensibly strict legal criteria as discussed above, the practical processes that determine the placement of children in secure units are something of a lottery, which may be influenced by any combination of four key factors.

First is the *vulnerability factor* itself. This applies to the child's particular circumstances and the degree to which they conform to the legal criteria relating to the restriction of liberty.

Second is the *professional agency factor*. This relates to the particular professional priorities of the lead agency involved with the child, together with the resources available to that agency. Thus Malek (1993: 87) found that despite 'common behaviour patterns' among 'children being removed from home', the precise nature of the 'factors affecting referral and the routes for admission into institutional care' were heavily influenced by agency-specific, as distinct from child-specific, priorities:

Each agency has its own terms for young people presenting behavioural problems but . . . whilst encompassing similar types of behaviour, nevertheless give them a particular focus. The justice system gives difficult behaviour a legal or criminal focus; within social services it is seen more in terms of parental control; the education system interprets it in relation to learning at school; and the psychiatric system provides a medical interpretation and diagnosis . . . The absence of any clear definitions permits young people to be dealt with in a number of different settings, because often their behaviour can be dealt with by any one of the four agencies . . . (Malek, 1993: 89)

The assessment, interpretation and formal 'diagnosis' of the child's behaviour, therefore, together with the particular response to it, is just as likely to be determined by the nature of the agency, its professional priorities and the significance that it attributes to the behaviour, as it is by the actual behaviour itself. Moreover, it is not only variations in specific professional priorities that will exercise such influence. Placement availability, together with the resources at the disposal of a particular agency at any given time, are also crucially significant and Malek concludes that:

> *This current study supports the view that the availability of provision influences where the young person is placed . . . The issue of funding influences placement decisions in a number of ways . . . a particular establishment may be deemed suitable but if no funding is available to meet the cost then admission will not occur.*
>
> *(ibid: 89–90)*

Third is the *structural location factor*, meaning the class, 'race' and gender of the child. Aymer and her colleagues make some very interesting observations in this respect:

> *. . . it became apparent that social class, race and gender played a significant part in determining the point of referral, the system into which the young people were inserted and their subsequent system careers. The more prosperous parents also tended to be white and they were unlikely to take their problems to the social services department. They would, instead, tend to consult their GP . . . Thus the young person, once inserted into a medical/psychiatric system would become a patient . . . The young people who entered secure accommodation by contrast, were, almost without exception, drawn from deprived working class families. Having a social worker and being in care are things which tend to happen only to the poorest people . . . and located within this group are a disproportionate number of black people. Once inserted into the system their careers run along familiar pathways, developing a peculiar logic and momentum, not least because the solution to the persistent breakdown of the institutional solution is, almost always, further institutionalisation. (Aymer et al., 1991: 97)*

In addition to class and race the child's gender is also a significant variable with regard to 'systems behaviour' and the nature of professional response. In this way welfare systems are disproportionately applied (both in scope and intensity) to girls (Goldson, 1997; Worrall, 1999). Consequently, although little or no difference has been found in rates of absconding between boys and girls for example (Wade *et al.*, 1998), the professional agencies are significantly more inclined to use heavy interventionist responses with girls who run away from children's homes and who are, as a direct result, far more likely than boys to be placed in secure accommodation via the welfare route (Goldson, 1992; Hodgkin, 1995; O'Neill, 2001).

Fourth is the *geographical variation factor*. This relates to inconsistencies in placing children in secure accommodation according to geographical location. In other words, it is the 'accident' (Dennington, 1991: 78) of where the child lives, the available resources within that area and the particular policies and practices of the local authority, which has significant influence on the likelihood of placement in secure accommodation. Hodgkin (1995) found quite staggering variations in such practices across different geographical areas, and O'Neill (1999: 290–291) has noted that 'it has been shown that the most powerful predictor of high admission rates is a local authority's ownership of a unit and that children are most likely to be placed in secure accommodation if they live in an authority which runs one'.

Irrespective of the legal criteria therefore, a range of ancillary factors exercise significant influence over the placement of children in secure accommodation. In turn, this suggests that the processes determining such placements are influenced by factors other than children's behaviour and considered professional judgement. This can only lead to the inappropriate placement of some children in secure settings and it is of little surprise that the secure unit managers who participated in Hodgkin's (1995: 4–5) study, for example, 'considered that 60 children out of 193 children surveyed could have been safely accommodated in open accommodation'. However, this concern cuts both ways and it is possible that the placement lottery not only serves to draw some children into secure accommodation inappropriately, but also denies others access to such units when a placement might be entirely appropriate and beneficial.

CONCERN 3: WHOSE PROTECTION? WHOSE INTERESTS?

Of all the children who enter secure accommodation by the welfare route, a significant proportion (especially of girls) have been assessed as vulnerable as a result of their involvement in prostitution and/or drug misuse. This raises significant problems and anxieties, not only for the children themselves, but also for the social work professionals who are charged with looking after them. Indeed, in such circumstances Social Services Departments face a 'damned if you do, damned if you don't' scenario. In other words, if they activate legal proceedings to restrict the liberty of the child in such circumstances, they may be criticised for over-zealous intervention. Alternatively, if they elect not to take such action they run the risk of even greater condemnation for failing to 'safeguard and promote the welfare of the child' especially if something should go dreadfully wrong. Individual careers are at stake here, as well as the reputation of the Social Services Department: secure accommodation is the 'safe option' irrespective of its value, or otherwise, to the child. In referring to these very circumstances Hodgkin has noted that:

> The primary reason for locking up such children was seen as political: that if they were not locked up social services risked being pilloried in the media. This was not to say that such children were not being damaged by the experiences or were not themselves very damaged individuals. But . . . the reasons why the children were locked up were . . . the care authority could not risk the consequences, not to the child but to itself. (Hodgkin, 1995: 30–31)

CONCERN 4: INEFFECTIVE SAFEGUARDS

A further concern relates to the limited effectiveness of the legal provisions and professional processes designed to safeguard children from unwarranted admissions to secure accommodation, and/or unnecessarily protracted periods of restricted liberty. There are three aspects to this concern.

First is the court process itself with regard to the welfare route into secure accommodation. Here the primary concern relates to the extent to which an application for a Secure Accommodation Order from a local authority is subjected to rigorous independent scrutiny by the Children's Guardian, the child's solicitor and the Family Proceedings bench. Despite apparently robust legal processes as outlined earlier in this chapter (*see* pp. 12–17), there are long-established anxieties that the courts essentially do little more than rubber-stamp such applications. Holden has noted that a 'care authority has little to fear from these procedures. The number of applications which have been refused have been very small' (cited in Dennington, 1991: 76). This point is highlighted further in an official consultation document published by the Department of Health at the time that the Children Act 1989 was due to be implemented: 'once the departmental decision has been made to "go for secure" there is a very good chance than an authorisation will be granted' (Department of Health, 1990).

Second is the difficult question of absconding. The criteria for admission to secure accommodation are provided by Section 25 of the Children Act 1989. Section 25 part 1(a) requires the court to be satisfied that the child has a 'history of absconding', is likely to abscond from 'any other description of accommodation' and if s/he absconds s/he is 'likely to suffer significant harm'. This appears to be relatively straightforward. However, there is no statutory definition of 'absconding' or 'a history of absconding' (Ashford and Chard, 2000: 248). Moreover, as Hodgkin's (1995: 26–28) study revealed, there is little professional consensus on what is meant by such terms.

Taking account of the other concerns that have been outlined above, the absconding criterion is likely to be easy to establish and there is little to safeguard the child in this respect. Indeed, children who 'abscond' from residential homes are, almost by definition, 'at risk': runaways are at risk because they run away, and which court is going to feel inclined to doubt that? What this does not take account of, however, is the *reason* for the child's running, which relates to the individual pathology *versus* systemic failure question. Furthermore, what we do know is that many children run from inadequate, if not abusive, residential homes (Stein *et al.*, 1994; Corby *et al.*, 2001) and why should they be locked up for that?

Third is the issue of the continued applicability of legal criteria once a child is placed in secure accommodation under the auspices of the welfare route. To reiterate, if the Family Proceedings Court is satisfied that the legal criteria apply, it is empowered to grant a Secure Accommodation Order for three months in the first instance and for six months on subsequent occasions. However, all such orders are permissive in that they enable, but do not oblige, the authority making the application to continue the placement (and thus keep the child locked up), for the full duration of the order. Indeed, official guidance explicitly states that 'a child must not continue to have his (*sic*) liberty restricted once the criteria cease to apply, even if there is a court order authorising restriction of liberty in existence' (Department of Health, 1993: para 8.27). Moreover, the same guidance provides that 'if at any stage the criteria for keeping the child in secure accommodation do not apply he should be released and put in alternative accommodation, as the court's authorisation is merely that – an authorisation' (*ibid*: para 8.9).

Again, all this appears to be clear and unproblematic especially given the formal processes for reviewing all such placements (*see* pp. 16–17). However, as noted earlier, despite the 'independent' element of the formal reviewing process, there is no obligation on the placing local authority, and/or the secure unit itself, to follow the recommendations of the reviewing panel. Furthermore, there is no legal provision allowing a child held in secure accommodation to apply to the court for leave to appeal, or to have their continued detention reviewed by the court itself. There are clear tensions between such practices on the one hand, and Article 37 of the United Nations Convention on the Rights of the Child and Article 5 of the European Convention on Human Rights (*see* pp. 18–20) on the other. Indeed, the circumscribed power of the reviewing process is a source of concern for children held in secure accommodation and for some professionals alike, and this issue will be explored further in Chapter 5.

CONCERN 5: PLACEMENT RHETORIC AND PRACTICE REALITY
Official guidance relating to secure accommodation claims that it 'has an important role to play' and emphasises the 'skills and enhanced levels of staff available, and the specialist programmes which can be provided'. Moreover, the same guidance continues:

It is important, in considering the possibility of a secure placement, that there is a clear view of the aims and objectives of such a placement and that those providing the accommodation can fully meet those aims and objectives . . . It is important that plans are made for continuity of care, education and, where appropriate, access to professional (e.g. psychiatric) support when the child leaves secure accommodation.

(Department of Health, 1993: para 8.5)

In other words, secure accommodation is presented as providing far more than restriction of liberty. Indeed, its 'important role' is conceived in terms of the added value that it is thought to provide by way of enhanced staff 'skills' and 'specialist programmes': it provides something that can not be provided elsewhere. Moreover, the guidance clearly states that the practice of placing children in secure units should take explicit account of the specific needs of the child, which should then be matched to the unit best placed to meet those needs. In this way, the secure unit placement is envisaged as part of a strategically managed therapeutic plan with a clear beginning, middle and end. The discussion above, particularly on the placement lottery, casts doubt over such rhetorical representation however, and it is of little surprise that O'Neill has observed that:

. . . care plans are frequently incomplete or missing altogether. Professionals under pressure are keen to get admissions but there is often a lack of proper planning about where the secure placement fits in the care plan, with no clear continuum of provision to facilitate transfer from locked to open accommodation. (O'Neill, 1999: 293)

There are two further concerns here. First, official guidance clearly has higher expectations of secure unit staff than is borne out by research evidence:

The complexity of the residential task in secure accommodation is unlikely to be adequately reflected in the qualifications of the staff . . . This study demonstrates that over 50 per cent of the sample of staff working in secure accommodation have no recognised professional training and/or qualification. It is likely that a national training/qualification audit of secure unit staff would reveal a substantially greater proportion of untrained and unqualified personnel . . . a substantial proportion of the staff sample reported having no previous experience of working with children . . . It is of some concern that staff with such limited experience and qualifications are required to work with children with diverse and formidable needs within the established complexities of secure accommodation. (Goldson, 1995: 12)

Second, there is very little research evidence available to suggest that secure accommodation fulfills the role that is expected of it. Vernon (1995: 2) asked 'what is the effect of security on young people?' for example, and could only conclude that 'despite the importance of this question, the relative absence of long-term studies means that there is a dearth of conclusive research evidence in this respect'. Furthermore, although Bullock and Little (1991: 2) noted that 'there is little doubt that secure accommodation is an effective damper on the immediate threat posed by difficult behaviour or grave danger', and that 'some observed improvements do seem to transfer to the outside world', they also advise that 'there are dangers of serious psychological and social damage being inflicted on children if placements are not managed well'. In other words, secure accommodation may provide limited benefit in certain circumstances, but it can also make bad problems worse in others: it can produce an iatrogenic effect.

CONCERN 6: A CURIOUS MIX

At the beginning of this chapter it was noted that secure accommodation draws its statutory authority from both civil and criminal statute and, as such, it fulfills specific functions within the child welfare system and the youth justice process. Consequently, children are placed in secure units under quite different (and arguably even contradictory) circumstances, and for equally different purposes: for *sanctuary* because they are thought to be especially vulnerable and in need of concentrated forms of care and protection; for *containment* in order to protect others, to deter them from offending and/or to guarantee that they attend court for trial or sentence; and for *punishment, retribution* and/or *rehabilitation* because they have been convicted of offences (ranging from the relatively minor to the most serious). In short, Dennington (1991: 90) refers to the 'bizarre admixture of young people' in secure units, some of whom are thought to be a danger to others while others are thought to be a danger to themselves (the latter category proportionately diminishing in size, as noted earlier). This inevitably raises complex questions about the true purpose of secure accommodation, its operational rationale, and its routines, regimes and practices. Such complexities are compounded further when we consider additional differentiating factors that apply to children in secure units:

> . . . the considerable differences in terms of the age, gender, ethnic origin . . . anticipated length of stay and distance from home area typify the profiles of children in secure facilities nationally. The implications that such differences raise in terms of managing and meeting the respective needs of such a 'mix' of children in closed facilities are profound . . . an intricate matrix of needs, rights and responsibilities calls for quite staggering versatility.
>
> (Goldson, 1995: 5)

Some commentators have highlighted the problems of such a diverse mix by emphasising incompatibility particularly along the (frequently gendered) 'offender' – 'non-offender' axis. Thus O'Neill (2001a: 6), reflecting on her research, comments upon the 'concern' of 'non-offenders' (particularly those who were known to have been sexually abused or working as prostitutes before admission) and the 'harmful emotional and physical effects of living alongside those convicted of violent and sexual offences of which they had been victims'. Similarly, Hodgkin (1995: 42), referring to girls with long histories of appalling sexual abuse and violation, questions how they 'could benefit from being locked up with convicted rapists and violent offenders'. Conversely, both O'Neill and Hodgkin, together with others, also acknowledge the similarities that such children share:

> Although secure units accommodate a diverse group of children who each have specific individual needs, similarities in their

> collective circumstances and requirements are striking. Most of
> the children in secure accommodation, irrespective of their legal
> status at the point of admission, have experienced unsettling and
> unstable family and domestic circumstances; chequered education;
> physical and/or sexual abuse; and invariably have poor self-images
> which are the net result of multiple disappointments and histories of
> failed relationships. The individual and collective needs of children
> within secure accommodation are compelling. (Goldson, 1995: 2)

The similarities shared by such children will be explored in Chapter 7. Equally, as noted earlier in this chapter, the welfare constituency of children within secure units represents a diminishing 'market share' of placements within secure accommodation as the justice constituency swells in size. This has significant implications regarding the mix of young people, a point that will be discussed further in Chapters 4 and 5.

CHAPTER *3*

Children in prison: remand law, policy and practice

Prisons collect [children] who find it difficult to cope, they collect excessive numbers of [children] with mental disorder, they collect [children] who have weak social supports, they collect [children] who, by any objective test, do not have rosy prospects. This collection of [children] is humiliated and stigmatised by the process of arrest, police inquiry and court appearance. [Child] prisoners suffer the ultimate ignominy of banishment to an uncongenial institution, which is often overcrowded, where friends cannot be chosen, and physical conditions are spartan. Above all, they are by the process separated from everything familiar, including all their social supports and loved ones, however unsatisfactory. This is what is supposed to happen, and this is what the punishment of prison is all about.

(Gunn, cited in Her Majesty's Chief Inspector of Prisons, 1999: 25)

The chaos that surrounds the treatment of children . . . in custody leads me to the conclusion that separate arrangements . . . are essential. Within this system children are, quite frankly, lost . . . From this review, and from inspection of establishments, I am convinced . . . that children should no longer be its responsibility.

(Her Majesty's Chief Inspector of Prisons, 1997: 70)

Dealing with youngsters on remand has proved one of the most difficult problems of criminal policy in recent years. Everyone agrees that jail is no place to hold unconvicted school children.

(Towler, 1999: 20)

PRISON REMANDS FOR CHILDREN: AN ENDURING PRACTICE

Despite the consistent array of concerns that have been raised (many from the most authoritative sources) on the practice of holding remanded children in prison custody, such practice persists. Although developments in law and policy throughout the 1970s, 1980s and early 1990s combined to restrict the remanding powers of the courts, substantial numbers of untried and/or convicted but unsentenced children continue to be held in prisons in England and Wales.

During this period the statutory power to remand children in prison was derived in the Children and Young Persons Act 1969, Section 23 of which allowed the court to remand a child if it considered that s/he was 'of so unruly a character that he (*sic*) cannot safely be committed to the care of the local authority'. However, it was not long before concerns were raised about the processes of 'unruliness certification' and the associated practice of prison remands. In 1975 the House of Commons Expenditure Committee, in its report *The Children and Young Persons Act 1969*, recommended that 'the practice of remanding young persons to adult prisons should cease forthwith' and that 'alternative arrangements must be made' (*see* Nacro, 1991). ·

Moreover, between 1976 and 1981 the powers of the courts to remand children to prison were incrementally restricted by legislation: 14-year-old girls were excluded from the procedure in 1977, 15- and 16-year-old girls were similarly excluded in 1979, as were 14-year-old boys in 1981 (Penal Affairs Consortium, 1996). Although the courts retained the power to remand 15- and 16-year-old boys to prison, the Parliamentary All-Party Penal Affairs Group, in its 1981 report *Young Offenders – A Strategy for the Future*, recommended that: '*a specific timetable should be announced for* ending the remand of 15 and 16 year olds in *Prison Department establishments* and rapid progress *should be made towards this objective*' (Parliamentary All-Party Penal Affairs Group cited in Nacro, 1991: my emphasis). Indeed, by the early 1980s the developing policy agenda appeared to offer genuine relief to those who shared a concern with the practice of juvenile penal remands, and the numbers of children entering prisons and remand centres in this way fell from 4812 in 1976 to 2059 in 1983. The pace of progress slowed by the mid-1980s. Although the Home Secretary, Leon Brittan, stated in 1984 that 'the government remains committed to . . . phasing out the remand to Prison Department establishments of unconvicted or unsentenced juveniles' (Brittan, cited in Nacro, 1988: 4), by 1988 the Earl of Caithness, Minister of State at the Home Office, commented: 'I regret to say that this undertaking has not yet been implemented' (*ibid*: 5). Moreover, despite the extraordinarily effective decarcerative policy and practice in respect of *sentenced* children during this period (Goldson, 1997a and 1999), such practice did not extend to *remanded* children in any such way. In other words, between 1984 and 1990 the numbers of children sentenced to prison custody fell consistently, year-on-year, producing a very substantial reduction (from 6500 to 1700), whereas the pattern in respect of juvenile penal remands fluctuated and although there was a decrease (from 1630 to 1263) it represented a far less dramatic decarcerative effect.

Table 4: Children sentenced and remanded to prison custody 1984–1990

Year	1984	1985	1986	1987	1988	1989	1990
Total sentenced[1]	6500	5900	4300	3900	3200	2300	1700
Total remanded[2]	1630	1638	1702	1861	1604	1459	1263

[1] Source: Newburn (1995: 138)
[2] Source: Nacro (1994: 8)

The early 1990s witnessed a renewed determination to address the issue of prison remands for children. In February 1991 the Home Office issued a consultation paper entitled *The Remand of Alleged Juvenile Offenders*, which contained two particularly significant proposals. First, it recommended that the practice of remanding children to prison custody should be reserved only for those cases where there 'was a need to protect the public from the risk of *serious harm*' (Home Office, cited in Penal Affairs Consortium, 1996: 2, my emphasis). Second, and more importantly, it proposed to make provision in the longer term for the complete abolition of prison remands for children. More significant still, each of the proposals were subsequently enshrined within Sections 60–62 of the Criminal Justice Act 1991, which received Royal Assent in October 1992. Indeed, in March 1992, Government circulars explained that:

> *The 1991 Act makes important changes to the arrangements for the remand of alleged offenders under 17 . . .*
>
> *– It abolishes unruliness as the test for a prison remand for 15 and 16 year old males, and replaces it with a test based on the need to protect the public from serious harm.*
>
> *– It provides for the eventual abolition of prison remands for 15 and 16 year old males, and the introduction of a new power for courts to remand direct to local authority secure accommodation 15 and 16 year olds who meet the new test for a prison remand. (This new power is referred to as a 'remand with a security requirement').*
>
> *(Home Office Circular 30/1992, Local Authority Circular LAC (92)5, Welsh Office Circular 21/92: para 45)*

This statutory provision for the complete abolition of prison remands for children was widely welcomed by penal reform, youth justice and child welfare organisations with two reservations. First, 17-year-old children were excluded, and, for the purposes of remand practice, would continue to be treated as adults. Second, the Government announced that the full implementation of the legislation would need to be suspended until there was sufficient secure accommodation available to replace prison custody. The 1991 Home Office consultation paper, *The Remand of Alleged Juvenile Offenders*, had estimated the likely demand for additional secure accommodation based upon an assumption that 'the number of juveniles remanded with a security requirement' would be 'considerably lower than the number remanded in Prison Department custody' and that 'a greater proportion of juveniles will be granted bail'. On this basis the Home Office projected that 'over the next four years it may be necessary to provide an extra *30 to 35 secure places* for juveniles on remand' (Home Office, cited in Penal Affairs Consortium, 1996: 3, my emphasis). However, the Government subsequently increased its estimate of the number of additional secure places required for this purpose to 65.

Despite these reservations, the Criminal Justice Act 1991 appeared to signal real progress to those who, for nearly 20 years, had consistently raised concerns about the practice of remanding children to prison. Few however, could have anticipated what was to follow, with a radical and reactionary shift in public mood and political priorities soon serving to dampen their optimism.

In late 1992 and early 1993 a fermenting body of opinion emerged that juvenile crime policy in particular, and penal liberalism in general, had gone 'too far'. Both the media and the police drew attention to car crime, youth disorder, children offending while on court bail ('bail bandits'), and those who they described as 'persistent young offenders', with increasing regularity and developing force. More detailed accounts of this mood of 'moral panic', its precipitating events, the political reactions to it and ultimately its impact on youth justice policy and practice can be found elsewhere (Goldson, 1997, 1999 and 2002; Muncie, 1999; Pitts, 2001). Suffice to say that the combined force of such processes witnessed the re-emergence of punitiveness, and ultimately a return to the increasing incapacitation and incarceration of children following a decade of developing decarcerative policies and practices. This had devastating consequences for prison remands for children.

In June 1993 the Association of Chief Probation Officers (ACOP) and NACRO published a report which showed that in the 12 months leading up to March 1993 the average daily number of children held on remand in prisons in England and Wales almost doubled (ACOP and Nacro, 1993). By January 1994 the Department of Health, realising that the projected expansion of secure accommodation would be woefully inadequate, wrote to local authority associations:

Since the estimate of 65 places was made, the Home Office and ourselves have considered again the number needed to abolish the practice of remanding 15 and 16 year old boys to prison. Given the scale on which the courts are currently remanding such defendants to the penal system, we consider that a total of 100 extra places will be necessary for implementation of s60 of the 1991 Act. Work is progressing at various stages to deliver these places. Our present estimate is that on present plans some of them will be ready in 1995, and the balance in 1996.

(Department of Health, cited in Penal Affairs Consortium, 1996: 4)

However, worse was yet to come. Within the context of moral panic, the 're-politicisation of youth crime' (Goldson, 1999: 7) and the emergence of a range of more punitive policy responses to children in trouble, the Criminal Justice and Public Order Act 1994 provided for the extension of 'remands with a security requirement' to include 12- to 14-year-olds. Thus the provisions of the Criminal Justice Act 1991, which had been introduced to facilitate the removal of 15- to 16-year-old boys from prison and the corresponding abolition of penal remands for such children, were paradoxically extended for the purposes of locking up a far younger constituency of school-age children. Consequently, the estimated necessary increase in the number of places within secure accommodation (which had started at 30–35 in 1991, had subsequently increased to 65 before again being inflated to 100 at the beginning of 1994) was once more revised to 170 in March 1994 (*see* p. 11). Moreover, the seemingly ever-increasing supply of secure accommodation made no tangible impact upon its ostensible primary purpose: to remove remanded 15- to 16-year-old boys from prison. In fact quite the opposite was seen to be true, and the prevailing punitive spirit produced a further increase in the numbers of 15- to 16-year-old boys being remanded to prison. The Audit Commission (1996: 31–32) observed that at the end of March 1996 the numbers of 15- to 17-year-olds in prison custody on remand was '20 per cent more than the year before' and this marked a general pattern which continued throughout the 1990s (Her Majesty's Chief Inspector of Prisons, 2000; Nacro, 1999; Nacro Cymru, 2000). In short, as Nacro (1998: 1) observed: 'the creation of 170 places in local authority secure accommodation has not proved sufficient to keep pace with an increase in the numbers of boys remanded to prison'.

There can be little doubt that the combined effect of the range of intensified and extended remand and sentencing powers relating to children – provided by the Criminal Justice and Public Order Act 1994, the Crime and Disorder Act 1998 and the Criminal Justice and Police Act 2001 (see pp. 42–44) – will continue to exacerbate the demand for secure accommodation and obstruct Section 60 of the Criminal Justice Act 1991 from realising its key objective: the abolition of prison remands for children. Indeed, the most recent developments in law and policy undermine this aim. On the one hand for example, Section 98 of the Crime and Disorder Act 1998 provides that a 15- to 16-year- old boy should not be remanded to prison custody if the court is 'of the opinion that, by virtue of his physical or emotional immaturity or a propensity of his to harm himself, it would be undesirable for [him] to be remanded to a prison'. On the other hand however, this ostensible safeguard is conditional upon the court having been 'notified that secure accommodation is available for him'. If no such accommodation is available, then the Act provides that the court – notwithstanding its explicit recognition of the child's vulnerability – 'shall remand him to a prison'. As already observed, such a scenario is likely to be common, meaning, as Ashton and Grindrod (1999: 188) had previously warned, that 'extremely damaged and vulnerable children will inevitably continue to be condemned to prison custody', thereby swelling what Medlicott (2001: 20) has termed 'the vast pool of vulnerability in prison'. If the 15- or 16-year-old boy is not judged to be 'vulnerable' however, then the court is at liberty to remand him to prison without needing to check the availability of secure accommodation. This also raises profound concerns with regard to the very conceptualisation of 'vulnerability', the means by which it is assessed, regional variations in such practice and the hostile conditions that confront *all children* remanded to prisons (see pp. 50–66, and Chapters 4 and 6).

The most recent statistical evidence is equivocal and the precise extent of prison remands for children is not entirely clear. Farrant (2001: 2) has noted that 'between April 2000 and April 2001 there was a seven per cent increase in the number of under 18-year-olds held in custody'. Elkins *et al.* (2001) survey Home Office figures for the June 2000–June 2001 period, which also record an increase in juvenile prisoners, although not as great as that indicated by Farrant. The sets of figures to which Farrant and Elkins *et al.* refer each relate to the *total* number of children in prison, both sentenced *and* remanded. For remand-only figures the current situation is even less clear. The Children's Society (2001: 4) has observed that 'the number of children on [prison] remand in England and Wales appears to have fallen' and this would concur with the *overall trend* relating to remanded 15- to 17-year-olds identified by Elkins and his colleagues (2001: 15). However, on closer analysis, their statistics also indicate a 21 per cent increase in 15-year-olds (arguably the most vulnerable group) being remanded into prison. What is clear, however, is that despite long-standing concerns and considerable abolitionist efforts over the past 25 years and more, the practice of remanding children in prisons has endured.

PRISON REMANDS FOR CHILDREN: THE LEGAL FRAMEWORK

There is a general right to bail for any child in criminal proceedings and all courts are legally obliged to consider granting bail at every hearing. However, further to such consideration bail may be refused and in such cases the court is initially guided by the Children and Young Persons Act 1969, which provides that:

where –

(a) a court remands a child or young person charged with or convicted of one or more offences or commits him for trial or sentence; and

(b) he is not released on bail,

the remand or committal shall be to local authority accommodation.

(Section 23(1), Children and Young Persons Act 1969)

Furthermore, in certain circumstances – when the conditions of Section 23(5) of the Children and Young Persons Act 1969 Act are satisfied – the court may make a *secure remand*. The criteria for a secure remand – as amended by the Crime and Disorder Act 1998 – are complicated and shall therefore be summarised here (for a more detailed discussion *see* Ashford and Chard, 2000; Moore and Smith, 2001).

The court may not declare that a child meets the criteria of Section 23(5) unless:

- s/he has attained the age of 12 years
- s/he is legally represented *and*
- the court has consulted with a probation officer or a social worker of a local authority Social Services Department.

The criteria comprise two parts:

Part *1* provides that the child must be:

- charged with, or have been convicted of, a violent or sexual offence, or an offence punishable in the case of an adult with imprisonment of fourteen years or more, *or*
- have a recent history of absconding while remanded to local authority accommodation, *and*
- be charged with, or convicted of, an imprisonable offence alleged or found to have been committed while s/he was so remanded.

Part 2 provides that:

- the court must be of the opinion that only remanding her/him to a remand centre or prison would be adequate to protect the public from serious harm from her/him.

Up until now, both parts of the criteria had to be satisfied before the court was able to subject the child to a secure remand. However, Section 130 of the Criminal Justice and Police Act 2001 provides for the relaxation of the secure remand criteria in a very important respect. Indeed, the Act empowers the courts to remand children to locked institutions in cases where they have committed 'repeat offences on bail' (Home Office, 2001), irrespective of whether or nor such offences are judged to expose the public to *serious harm* (Roberts, 2001). This effectively replaces the seriousness threshold with a nuisance test as Jack Straw, the then Home Secretary, originally explained:

> There have been a number of cases where young 'bail bandits' have repeatedly committed offences when on bail. The courts currently lack the power to remand them to custody unless they commit a more serious offence, effectively allowing persistent young offenders to 'thumb their noses' at the law . . . It is simply

> *not acceptable that the courts have no powers to remand those*
> *juvenile offenders to custody.*
> *(Straw cited in Home Office, 2001: 1–2)*

It is inevitable that, when implemented, the new provisions of the Criminal Justice and Police Act 2001 will swell the numbers of children remanded to secure accommodation and prison and exacerbate the strain on the juvenile secure estate (*see* pp. 83–85). As such it was widely believed that the implementation of Section 130 would be stalled until additional capacity was provided. However, in an unexpected announcement in April 2002, David Blunkett (who replaced Straw after the General Election of 2001), stated that the new powers were to be implemented immediately (Travis, 2002: 1).

In the case of boys aged 12–14 and girls aged 12–16, secure remand is direct to secure accommodation. In most cases boys aged 15–16 will be remanded to prison. However, as discussed above, Section 98 of the Crime and Disorder Act 1998 amends the Children and Young Persons Act 1969 with regard to 15- and 16-year-old boys by providing that the court *may* remand such children to secure accommodation as an alternative to prison if:

• it is of the opinion that, by reason of his physical or emotional immaturity or a propensity of his to harm himself, it would be undesirable for him to be remanded to prison, *and*
• it is notified that a bed in a secure unit is available.

In practice, however, as already observed, this 'safeguard' is both relatively ineffective (given the excessive demand for, and limited supply of, secure unit places), and deeply problematic given the vulnerability of *all* such children within the prison environment. However, before turning attention to this latter point it is worth briefly considering the provisions of statute, conventional obligations, international standards, treaties and rules in respect of the rights of children remanded to prison custody.

PRISON REMANDS AND CHILDREN'S RIGHTS

Bearing in mind the discussion so far in this chapter, together with what follows on key concerns relating to children remanded in prisons, the very concept of children's rights and prison remands seems to be an oxymoron. Indeed, it was the Right Honourable Lord Justice Woolf and His Honour Judge Stephen Tumin who observed that 'a prisoner, as a result of being in prison, is particularly vulnerable to arbitrary and unlawful action' (Woolf, 1991), and Chesney *et al.* (2000: 144) have even questioned whether or not rights-based instruments 'make the slightest bit of difference behind prison walls'.

Despite such reservations, Her Majesty's Chief Inspector of Prisons has recently reminded us that the provisions of statute, conventional obligations, international standards, treaties and rules 'establish particular protections and rights for young people in detention (a) because they are in detention and (b) because they have not reached adult age' (Her Majesty's Chief Inspector of Prisons, 1997: 82). Such 'protections and rights', together with the legal instruments that confer them, deserve attention: a review follows of the United Nations Standard Minimum Rules for the Administration of Juvenile Justice, the United Nations Convention on the Rights of the Child and the Human Rights Act 1998 relating to children remanded into prisons.

UNITED NATIONS STANDARD MINIMUM RULES FOR THE
ADMINISTRATION OF JUVENILE JUSTICE (BEIJING RULES)
The Beijing Rules were adopted by the United Nations in 1985 and provide guidance for the protection of children's rights in the development of separate and specialist juvenile justice systems. They were a direct response to a call made by the Sixth United Nations Congress on the Prevention of Crime and the Treatment of Offenders, which convened in 1980. The Rules operate within a framework of two other sets of rules governing juvenile justice, both of which were adopted in 1990: The United Nations Guidelines for the Prevention of Juvenile Delinquency (the Riyadh Guidelines), and the United

Nations Rules for the Protection of Juveniles Deprived of their Liberty (the JDL Rules).

Many of the Beijing Rules apply to children remanded in prisons, examples of which include:

- Rule 1.1, which provides that 'Member States shall seek, in conformity with their respective general interests, to further the well-being of the juvenile and her or his family'

- Rule 1.3, which provides that 'sufficient attention should be given to positive measures that involve the full mobilisation of all possible resources . . . for the purpose of promoting the well-being of the juvenile, with a view to reducing the need for intervention under the law, and of effectively, fairly and humanely dealing with the juvenile in conflict with the law'

- Rule 2.1, which provides that 'the following Standard Minimum Rules shall be applied to juvenile offenders impartially, without distinction of any kind, for example as to race, colour, sex, language, religion'

- Rule 13.1, which provides that 'detention pending trial shall be used only as a measure of last resort and for the shortest possible period of time'

- Rule 13.3, which provides that 'juveniles under detention pending trial shall be entitled to all rights and guarantees of the Standard Minimum Rules for the Treatment of Prisoners adopted by the United Nations'

- Rule 13.5, which provides that 'while in custody, juveniles shall receive care, protection and all necessary individual assistance . . . that they may require'

- Rule 19.1, which provides that 'the placement of a juvenile in an institution shall always be a disposition of last resort and for the minimum necessary period'

- Rule 22.1, which provides that 'professional education [and] in-service training . . . shall be utilised to establish and maintain the necessary professional competence of all personnel dealing with juvenile cases'

As discussed in Chapter 2, the United Nations Convention on the Rights of the Child – the first detailed international treaty to provide comprehensive minimum standards for the treatment of all children – was ratified by the UK Government in December 1991. Although the Articles of the UN Convention apply to *all children*, some are particularly relevant to the circumstances of children held on remand in prisons including:

• Article 1, which provides that 'a child means every human being below the age of eighteen years' (this is particularly interesting with regard to the treatment of 17-year-old children in remand proceedings in England and Wales – *see* pp. 52–53)

• Article 2, which provides for non-discrimination, not unlike Rule 2.1 of the Beijing Rules (this is pertinent to institutionalised racism within prisons and the wider youth justice system – *see* pp. 55–56)

• Article 3, which provides for the best interests of the child consistent with Rules 1.1, 1.3 and 13.5 of the Beijing Rules (this jars with the conditions and treatment of children in prisons – *see* pp. 50–52)

• Article 6, which provides (at 6.1) that State Parties 'recognise that every child has the inherent right to life', and (at 6.2) that they 'shall ensure to the maximum extent possible the survival and development of the child' (this is particularly pertinent to the incidence of self-harm and suicide on prison remand wings for children – *see* pp. 59–63)

• Article 19, which provides for the protection of the child from 'all forms of physical and mental violence, injury or abuse, neglect or negligent treatment, maltreatment or exploitation', similar to Rule 13.5 of the Beijing Rules (this is applicable to the conditions and treatment of children in prison, cultures of bullying, and again incidence of self-harm and suicide – *see* pp. 58–63)

• Article 24, which provides for the child's highest attainable standard of health (this concerns children's health and the provision of health care in prisons – *see* pp. 56–58)

- Article 27, which provides for the child's right to benefit from an adequate standard of living (a right routinely withheld for the overwhelming majority of children in trouble – *see* pp. 50–52 and pp. 153–154)
- Articles 28 and 29, which provide for the child's right to education (a further right apparently denied to many children in conflict with the law – *see* p. 51 and p. 154)

Perhaps most relevant of all are Articles 37 and 40, which both raise fundamental issues relating to the treatment of children in prisons. However, both these Articles, and the principles they express, sit very uncomfortably alongside the realities of children's experiences of prison remand, as seen below and in Chapter 6.

- Article 37 provides that 'no child shall be subjected to . . . cruel, inhuman or degrading treatment . . . imprisonment of a child shall be . . . used only as a measure of last resort and for the shortest appropriate period of time . . . every child deprived of liberty shall be treated with humanity and respect for the inherent dignity of the human person'.
- Article 40 provides that 'States Parties recognise the right of every child alleged as, accused of, or recognised as having infringed the penal law to be treated in a manner consistent with the promotion of the child's sense of dignity and worth'.

THE HUMAN RIGHTS ACT 1998

As noted in Chapter 2, the Human Rights Act came into effect in October 2000 and requires all other domestic legislation to be compatible with the European Convention on Human Rights (ECHR). Unlike the United Nations Convention on the Rights of the Child and the United Nations Standard Minimum Rules for the Administration of Juvenile Justice, the ECHR was not compiled specifically with children in mind, although increasingly the European Court's rulings have acknowledged the special vulnerabilities of children. Moreover, now that the Human Rights Act 1998 has been implemented, any child who believes that their rights have been violated by a *public authority* will have redress before a UK court. This could be a very significant development and

Levenson (2000: 1) has claimed that the Human Rights Act 'has the potential to be one of the most important constitutional changes [in] 300 years'.

As a 'public authority' the Prison Service is now obliged to comply with the provisions of the Human Rights Act and to respect the rights and freedoms that it confers. However, Levenson (*ibid*: 1 and 4) believes that 'many of the Prison Service's policies and practices are in danger of violating the Act' and it 'is likely to be challenged under almost every article'. Even the most cursory analysis of some of the Articles (which might apply to children remanded in prison) would seem to confirm this view.

• Article 2 provides that everyone's right to life shall be protected by law (as stated above in relation to Articles 6 and 19 of the UN Convention on the Rights of the Child and associated Beijing Rules, the question of self-harm and suicide may well be raised in this respect).

• Article 3 provides that no one should be subjected to torture or to inhuman or degrading treatment or punishment (this echoes Articles 37 and 40 of the UN Convention on the Rights of the Child and will no doubt prompt discomforting questions in relation to the treatment, conditions and regime cultures encountered by child remand prisoners).

• Article 8 provides that everyone has the right to respect for their private and family life which arguably has particular applicability in the case of children (this becomes problematic for the many children who are held on remand in prisons at considerable distance from their family homes and communities making visits from parents, carers and other family members extraordinarily difficult).

• Article 14 provides for freedom from discrimination (again this is consistent with Article 2 of the UN Convention on the Rights of the Child and Rule 2.1 of the Beijing Rules, but it has a particularly hollow ring alongside the endemic presence of racism within prisons in particular, and the youth justice system in general – *see* pp. 55–56 and Goldson, 2001; Goldson and Chigwada-Bailey, 1999; Goldson and Peters, 2000).

There is an obvious tension between the language of child rights and the practice of child imprisonment. Such tension is clearly expressed by contrasting the rights provisions that have been considered above, with the concerns that are identified below and throughout Chapter 6. Moreover, within this context, both the efficacy and justice of the remedies available to children in prison might need to be questioned. Here the vulnerability of the child remand prisoner is particularly stark. Ultimately a 15- to 16-year-old boy's right to redress in respect of his treatment *within* the prison is a prison matter: the child essentially stands alone against the full power of the system. How must a child feel in such circumstances? Can there be a greater sense of powerlessness and vulnerability? Is the pretence that such children have rights and that these rights are found within a system of justice truly acceptable?

CHILDREN IN PRISON: SOME CONCERNS ABOUT PENAL REMANDS

> *Of all the parts of the Prison Service that we inspect, the one that gives all of us in the Inspectorate greatest cause for concern is the Young Prisoner estate.*
>
> *(Her Majesty's Chief Inspector of Prisons, 1997: 3)*

> *The picture for young prisoners on remand . . . is extreme . . . These statistics describe a group of young people . . . isolated, victimised and disturbed. Many of them have experienced significant trauma and disruption in their domestic lives and their schooling, and are without the personal and social support they need to overcome their difficulties and begin to manage their lives and relationships. Many are mentally, emotionally and morally immature . . . Before any work can be done to sensitise them to the needs of others and the impact of their offending on victims, their own needs as maturing adolescents for care, support and direction have to be met.*
>
> *(Her Majesty's Chief Inspector of Prisons, 2000: 25)*

As discussed earlier in this chapter (*see* pp. 35–39), concern regarding the practice of remanding children in prisons has substantial antecedent. In more recent years Her Majesty's Chief

Inspector of Prisons has produced numerous reports that comprise the most compelling body of evidence suggesting that such concern is as apposite today as it has ever been. Taken together with research findings and practice experience, the evidence is unequivocal. Children whose lives have been damaged and disfigured by disadvantage, neglect and abuse are the very children who occupy the juvenile remand wings of our prisons. These are children for whom the fabric of life invariably stretches across poverty; family discord; public care; drug and alcohol misuse; mental distress; ill-health; emotional, physical and sexual abuse; self-harm; homelessness; isolation; loneliness; circumscribed educational and employment opportunities; and the most pressing sense of distress and alienation. Such children are, in many important respects, 'discarded' (Her Majesty's Chief Inspector of Prisons, 1999: 23) and 'treated like rubbish' (Lyon *et al.*, 2000: 29). Moreover, despite an apparent fall in juvenile crime in recent years, the numbers of children entering prisons and other locked institutions (both as remand and sentenced prisoners) has continued to rise (Goldson, 2002). Much of this has been driven by political posturing (Pitts, 2000 and 2001); very little is the product of rational youth justice practice (Goldson, 2001a); yet all of it serves to impose further damage upon already damaged children (Goldson and Peters, 2000).

Such children are profoundly vulnerable. They are placed in institutions singularly unsuited to their needs (Goldson and Peters, 2000), and invariably at great distance from their home areas (Her Majesty's Chief Inspector of Prisons, 2000: 115). The safeguards, protections and rights that are conferred by international conventions, standards, treaties and rules have limited application in practice (as discussed above), and the primary piece of child welfare legislation – the Children Act 1989 – much to the dismay of Her Majesty's Inspectorate of Prisons, does not even apply to the prison estate (Her Majesty's Chief Inspector of Prisons, 1997: 6; Her Majesty's Chief Inspector of Prisons, 2001: 8). Children remanded in prisons are therefore exposed, with only the most limited forms of protection, to hostile conditions and 'sink-or-swim' sub-cultures underpinned by 'belief rules' such as: 'do not rely on anybody other than yourself'; 'take your time working out who you can trust'; 'be especially wary of Prison Officers' and 'keep your head down' (Her Majesty's Chief Inspector of Prisons, 1997: 17). Some children apparently survive more or less intact; others don't. Increasingly 'vulnerability assessments' are implemented and applied to identify and screen-out the 'most vulnerable' (*see* pp. 72–83 and pp. 134–140). However, there are both practical and conceptual problems with such processes. On the one hand they are extraordinarily difficult to execute accurately, as discussed later (*see* pp. 63–64). On the other:

> 'Coping' classifications belong to the language of a psychiatric/ pathology model, and can serve to neutralise the very real problems that *all* [child] prisoners have in adapting to the prison environment. They obscure the fundamental recognition of the environment as essentially problematic. In practice, they legitimise awarding special attention to some prisoners and withholding it from others.
>
> (Medlicott, 2001: 26, my emphasis)

The over-riding concern here is that *all* children in prison are vulnerable and while the practice of differentiating vulnerabilities, and/or constructing hierarchies of vulnerability, is understandable as a pragmatic response, it detracts attention from the inherent unsuitability of the prison *per se*. The elements of this broad concern are articulated by many of the professionals and children interviewed during the research for this book. Their accounts are expressed in Chapter 6 but some of the documentary evidence shall be reviewed here.

CONCERN 1: THE 'ADULT-CHILD'?

It has already been noted that the Children Act 1989 does not apply in prisons that stand 'on Crown property [thus] allowing immunity' (Her Majesty's Chief Inspector of Prisons, 2001a: 18). Indeed, Her Majesty's Chief Inspector of Prisons has commented elsewhere that:

> I recommend that the application of the Children Act 1989 be reviewed, particularly with such large numbers of children being held in Prison Service custody since the Act was passed. The Prison Service asserts that Governors of establishments holding Young Prisoners are neither in loco parentis, nor are they guardians . . .

If this is correct it also raises the question of who is in loco parentis,
and if it is not the Governor, who is it?

(Her Majesty's Chief Inspector of Prisons, 1997: 21)

So the child remand prisoner is not only denied the protection of child welfare legislation but is seemingly also cut adrift from the guardianship and care of an identifiable adult. The situation for the 17-year-old child is worse still.

The Children Act 1989 and the United Nations Convention on the Rights of the Child define the child as 'every human being below the age of 18 years'. Despite this, the 17-year-old child is regarded as an adult for the purposes of remand policy and practice:

Although the Criminal Justice Act 1991 extended the age range of
the renamed youth courts it created an anomaly . . . by treating
17 year olds differently to the younger age range . . . In relation to
bail and remands, 17 year olds are treated as though they were
adults. (Ashford and Chard, 2000: 227)

In other words, the 17-year-old boy has his very claim to childhood denied. In turn this serves to remove such children from the reach of Section 60 of the Criminal Justice Act 1991 (which provides for the abolition of prison remands, as discussed above), and from Section 98 of the Crime and Disorder Act 1998 (which obliges the court to consider the question of vulnerability before remanding a child in prison, also discussed above).

CONCERN 2: UNJUST REMANDS, UNJUST TREATMENT

As discussed earlier, Section 23(5) of the Children and Young Persons Act 1969 provides that before a court may remand a child to prison it must be of the opinion that such action is *necessary* in order to protect the public from *serious harm*. However, for many years there has been ample evidence to suggest that children who pose no such risk are routinely held in prisons on remand. In 'interpreting the facts' Nacro (1994: 10) concluded that 'it seems likely that custody is not essential for all those currently remanded', and more recently The Children's Society (2001: 11) has reported that 'around one-quarter of the children' surveyed by the National Remand Review Initiative during a 12-month period 'were remanded [in prisons] for property offences'. Indeed, Her Majesty's Chief Inspector of Prisons (2000: 20) has commented upon the very substantial number 'of prisoners held on remand [who] do not receive a custodial sentence'. After analysing the court disposals in relation to 603 children who had been held in prison on remand The Children's Society (2001: 19) noted that 'around one-third of children received community sentences after the period on remand [and] a further 5.6 per cent of children had their charges withdrawn or were found not guilty'. Taken together, analyses of pre-remand offences and post-remand sentences suggest that substantial numbers of children are being held in prisons unnecessarily and unjustly in relation to the 'serious harm' criteria. Moreover, once Section 130 of the Criminal Justice and Police Act 2001 is fully implemented, such numbers will inevitably multiply.

There are also concerns about the geographical variations in penal remand practice. A recent survey in Wales for example, revealed that 'remand into custody rates vary significantly across each local authority' (Nacro Cymru, 2000: 2). Having studied 506 remand case returns from 19 local authorities in Wales, the researchers found that some authorities produced no custodial remands while others produced almost three times the average. Similar patterns in England have been attributed to inconsistent remand/sentencing cultures within and between the courts, and the varying quality of remand management and bail support services made available by local Youth Offending Teams (Goldson, Peters and Simkins, 2001; Goldson and Peters, 2002).

The influence of geographical variation is not, however, limited to the determination of court process. Indeed, children who are remanded in prisons are subject to a second-tier geographical effect, which can exercise significant influence over the quality of the custodial experience itself. Her Majesty's Chief Inspector of Prisons has noted:

> As I have inspected establishments holding similar types of prisoner, I have become more and more aware of, and concerned about, inconsistencies between them in the treatment and conditions

of prisoners . . . The treatment of young prisoners is something of a lottery, because it depends on conditions available in the establishment in which they are confined as well as different attitudes towards them amongst some staff. This means that the few really good establishments, where young offenders are treated properly, stand out in sharp contrast to the majority.

(Her Majesty's Chief Inspector of Prisons, 1997: 3–4)

Indeed, more recently Her Majesty's Chief Inspector (2001: 10) has drawn attention to 'the inconsistency in treatment and conditions' for children in Young Offender Institutions, some of which 'have produced excellent examples for others to follow' whereas in others 'set alongside them . . . are the horrors that we found'.

CONCERN 3: ENDEMIC RACISM

Despite the legal duty that applies to all 'persons engaged in the administration of criminal justice' to 'avoid discriminating against any persons on the grounds of race' (Section 95(1)(b) Criminal Justice Act 1991) – together with the non-discrimination provisions of international conventions, standards, treaties and rules discussed above – racism is endemic throughout the youth justice system (Goldson, 1999a; Goldson and Chigwada-Bailey, 1999). This 'corrosive disease' (Macpherson, 1999: para 6.34) not only means that black children are more likely (than their white counterparts) to be remanded in custody, but they also face the prospect of less favourable treatment and conditions.

Indeed, Ashton and Grindrod (1999: 177) have reflected upon the 'hugely disproportionate use of prison custody being made in respect of black children . . . which was particularly marked in the case of those remanded to custody', and similar findings have been reported by Goldson and Peters (2000) and The Children's Society (2001). Moreover, the Director General of the Prison Service has recently acknowledged that the prison system is 'institutionally racist' (cited in Goldson, 2001: 19), and Her Majesty's Chief Inspector of Prisons has commented:

I have long been concerned that the biggest single problem facing the Director General is the culture that still pervades parts of the prison system . . . It is a culture that adopts an attitude to prisoners that is not only judgmental, but too often includes physical and mental brutality . . . One of its most obvious manifestations is in attitudes to minorities, of whatever kind, who are treated not as equal but as unequal because of their minority status. There are . . . minority groups whose inequality of treatment concerns me – ethnic or cultural minorities.

(Her Majesty's Chief Inspector of Prisons, 2001: 16)

What this amounts to is a form of racialised compound vulnerability: vulnerable black children facing an increased likelihood of penal remand, and the associated prospect of hostile treatment and conditions, on the basis of their minority ethnic status alone.

CONCERN 4: UNHEALTHY PRISONS

Her Majesty's Chief Inspector of Prisons (2000: 63) has noted that 'surprisingly little is known about the physical health of unsentenced prisoners'. What is known, however, does not paint a very encouraging picture. Indeed, in one survey 26 per cent of young remand prisoners were found to be taking prescribed medication before being sent to custody (*ibid*: 65), and Her Majesty's Chief Inspector has observed elsewhere that 'a very significant proportion of the population of young people in custody need help with health care . . . adolescents in custody represent a concentration of unhealthy lifestyles, reflecting the need for advice and care related to a range of health issues' (Her Majesty's Chief Inspector of Prisons, 1997: 45). Similarly, the British Medical Association (2001: 1 and 5), commenting upon the relationship between poverty, disadvantage and poor health, has noted: 'patients within prison are amongst the most needy in the country in relation to their health care needs. Over 90 per cent of patients who reside in our jails come from deprived backgrounds . . . 17 per cent of young offenders were not registered with a general practitioner and generally the young people had a low level of contact with primary health care'.

More is known about the mental health of children and young people in prison and Her Majesty's Chief Inspector of Prisons (1997: 45) has noted that 'over 50 per cent of young prisoners on remand

and 30 per cent of sentenced young offenders have a diagnosable mental disorder'. Lader *et al.* (2000), in their wide-ranging study of 'psychiatric morbidity' among children and young people in prison found that 84 per cent of remand prisoners had a 'personality disorder'; eight per cent had a psychotic disorder; 60 per cent had sleep problems; 70 per cent had 'hazardous drinking' habits; 93 per cent reported using drugs before remand; and 'male young offenders on remand were the most likely to report having suffered . . . stressful life events'. Moreover, and not surprisingly, the experience of imprisonment itself has been identified as having a deleterious effect on the mental well-being of children and young people (Her Majesty's Chief Inspector of Prisons 1997; Farrant, 2001; Leech and Cheney, 2001; Mental Health Foundation, 1999).

Taken together, the physical and mental health needs of children held on remand in prisons are such to require sustained attention from an expertly staffed and well-resourced range of health services. But, the reality is quite different:

> *The Prison Service is being consistently starved of adequate funding to meet this clinical and social care agenda . . . the prison medical service has been in an acute crisis for some time . . . because of the general shortage of resources in prisons, prison medical officers often have inadequate support from an appropriately qualified healthcare team . . . unqualified 'hospital officers' are given responsibility for aspects of clinical care that in the NHS would only be given to clinical staff with appropriate training.*
>
> *(British Medical Association, 2001: 1–2)*

The prison health care service is not formally part of the National Health Service and, despite the fact that Her Majesty's Chief Inspector of Prisons (1996) has recommended that responsibility for health care in prisons should be transferred to the NHS, this has yet to happen. Despite the best efforts of health care staff in prisons, children who have compelling health-related needs are exposed to environments in which their health is likely to deteriorate further. They are consequently left with a second-rate service which is 'not equipped to meet their needs' (Her Majesty's Chief Inspector of Prisons, 2000: 69–70).

CONCERN 5: SYSTEMIC BULLYING

It has long been known that bullying is rife in Young Offender Institutions. This is now officially acknowledged, and many formal attempts are being made to address it through the development of anti-bullying strategies and a more sensitised awareness of child protection:

Children are made worse by the experience of imprisonment [and] the bullying and harassment that they inflict on each other . . . The emphasis on Child Protection procedures should be not so much on children being molested by staff, although this must, of course, be guarded against, but on protecting them from bullying and intimidation by their peers when staff are not present. The worst examples of this are reflected in establishments where verbal intimidation is practiced by shouting from cells, and physical bullying takes place in unsupervised places such as showers and recesses on landings. It is essential that all parts of establishments holding children and young adults are made safe, so that the ravages of bullying and intimidation cannot be wrought.

(Her Majesty's Chief Inspector of Prisons, 2001: 9)

Indeed, the staff from every Young Offender Institution visited during the research for this book were keen to emphasise the efforts that were being made to combat bullying. However, many doubted the practical efficacy of such effort and, during the interviews, staff and children alike confirmed that bullying remains widespread (*see* pp. 143–148).

Bullying takes many forms in prisons holding children. Perhaps the most obvious example is physical assault, much of which goes unreported, and thus unrecorded, owing to the intense antipathy to the practice of 'grassing' and, worse still, the risks associated with being labelled a 'grass'. Despite this, in one Young Offender Institution alone, 222 assaults were recorded in a 12-month period between 2000 and 2001, giving an assault rate of 93 per cent (the rate of assault is measured by the number of proven adjudications of assault as a percentage of the average prisoner population) (Howard League, 2001: 8). There can be no doubt that physical assault is commonplace. However, children are also exposed to other forms of bullying including sexual assault; verbal abuse (name-calling, threats, racist taunting); extortion and theft; and lending and trading cultures – particularly in relation to tobacco – involving extraordinary rates of interest, which accumulate daily.

Bullying is also extremely difficult to identify; it may be transmitted by no more than a look-in-the-eye, and with staff-child ratios so stretched within prisons, levels of supervision are inevitably thin. Moreover, bullying is contagious. It is entrenched within the fabric of prison life; it is integral to the very incivility of child imprisonment and it is an intrinsic feature of the survival-of-the-fittest machismo that prevails. The bullied child is invariably also a bully; the damaged wreak damage as the victim becomes the aggressor within the corrosive environment that is prison. Medlicott captures this phenomenon eloquently:

This is the self who knows he has always fought for things and caused trouble, who needs love in order to grasp at a feeling of safety which has eluded him all his life, who does bad things to himself and to others because he is a bad and evil person, who has been so troubled by feeling unsafe all his life that he grasps greedily at every bit of power that comes his way. This self has a tender and caring side, but not one that can be sustained. Threatened with pain, even if only in the form of hurtful remarks, this is a self that lashes out. (Medlicott, 2001: 172)

It is of little surprise that within this culture of torment, children's vulnerabilities are compounded and exposed. For all, bullying perpetuates misery and fear. For some, it is literally too much to bear.

CONCERN 6: ULTIMATE VULNERABILITY – SELF-HARM AND SUICIDE

It is widely acknowledged that the incidence of self-harm and the number of suicides in prisons in England and Wales has increased very substantially over the last decade or more (Liebling, 1996; McHugh and Snow, 2000; Neal, 1996). It is also accepted that the official statistics do not provide an accurate measure of the *actual* depth and extent of self-harm and suicidal intent in prisons, much of which goes unrecorded (Howard League, 1999; Liebling and Krarup,

1993; Medlicott, 2001). Despite the practice of under-recording and the associated deficiencies of official data however, the statistics that are available present a harrowing picture of self-inflicted damage and lost life. Between 1994 and 1997 for example, there were 4212 reported incidents of deliberate self-harm in Young Offender Institutions in England and Wales (*see* Table 5). This averages just under four incidents every day of every week for the entire three-year period. Moreover, during the 1990–2000 period 134 children and young people took their own lives in prisons, 54 of whom were remand prisoners (*see* Table 6). Indeed, the combination of youth, remand and prison can quite literally be lethal.

Table 5: Reported incidents of self-harm in prisons in England and Wales (young people aged 15–21 years)

Year	1994–1995	1995–1996	1996–1997	Three-year total
Reported incidents	1216	1823	1173	4212

Source: Her Majesty's Inspectorate of Prisons (1997)

Table 6: Suicides in prisons in England and Wales (young people aged 15–21 years) 1990–2000

Year	Sentenced	Remanded	Total
1990	4	6	10
1991	4	1	5
1992	4	6	10
1993	3	0	3
1994	5	7	12
1995	8	4	12
1996	4	10	14
1997	12	4	16
1998	11	4	15
1999	14	5	19
2000	11	7	18

Source: Inquest (2001)

Kerfoot (2000) reports that suicide is now the second most common cause of death among young people generally, and since the 1970s suicide rates have shown a particular increase in respect of 15- to 19-year-old males. Furthermore, Kerfoot (*ibid*) illustrates that within this age group there is a clear correlation between family, social and economic disadvantage, and susceptibility to suicide and self-harm. It is, as has already been acknowledged, precisely such circumstances that invariably define the lives of children remanded in prison. Indeed, when the pressures of prison life (within which bullying and intimidation are prominent) begin to bear down upon such children, their vulnerabilities are inevitably exposed and compounded. It is of little surprise therefore, that Inquest (2000: 1) has noted that 'juvenile prisoners are the group most at risk of suicide and self-harm', a crucial point which has also been made by others (Liebling, 1996; Lader *et al.*, 2000).

For children held in prisons on remand, vulnerability is further intensified by their very remand status. Dooley (1990) for example, analysed 300 suicides among prisoners over a 15-year period and found that those on remand were particularly high risk. Earlier international research has also confirmed that remand prisoners are consistently over-represented in prison suicide figures (Backett, 1987; Hatty and Walker, 1986; Home Office, 1984; Novick and Remmlinger, 1978). Indeed, the particular vulnerabilities of child remand prisoners are now well-recognised. This is especially so on their first night in prison and the very early part of their prison experience (Bogue and Power, 1995; Her Majesty's Chief Inspector of Prisons, 1999), and many of the children and professionals who were interviewed in the research for this book expressed this point with exceptional clarity (*see* Chapter 6).

Her Majesty's Chief Inspector of Prisons has observed:

Young people in prison are more vulnerable and impulsive than most adults. Young people in general and young prisoners in particular (and those on remand even more so) are impulsive, uncertain and changeable . . . Young offenders often have limited understanding of the consequences of their actions and little sense of future . . .

Any death by suicide is devastating, the untimely death of a child or young person seems particularly tragic.

(Majesty's Chief Inspector of Prisons, 1999: 39)

It is difficult to imagine what goes through a child's mind in prison. It is even more difficult to understand what drives a boy to deliberately harm himself, or worse, to take his own life, while he is being held in prison on remand. As Medlicott (2001: 5) has noted, the children best placed to illuminate our understanding are dead. Edwin Schneidman provides some insight, however:

It is the words that suicidal people say – about their pain and frustrated needs – that make up the essential vocabulary of suicide . . . Suicidal death is an escape from pain . . . Pain is Nature's great signal . . . it both mobilises us and saps our strength; pain, by its very nature, makes us want to stop it or escape from it . . .
Everyone who commits suicide feels driven to it – indeed feels that suicide is the only option left.

(Schneidman, cited in Her Majesty's Chief Inspector of Prisons, 1999: 19)

It is painful to even attempt to understand the desperate emotional angst of the child who 'feels that suicide is the only option left', and yet there are many children in our prisons who are left with such thoughts. Lader *et al.* (2000: 34) have recently noted that almost 40 per cent of young male remand prisoners in their research sample reported to having considered suicide at some stage in their life, and ten per cent had considered such action within a week before their interview.

Some commentators have argued that prisons are no place for children (*see*, for example, Goldson and Peters, 2000), but despite the considerable weight of evidence substantiating this view, it remains largely unheard within the current penal policy climate. In the meantime others suggest a more pragmatic approach:

[Children] in custody are peculiarly vulnerable and dependent . . .
I shall take those arguments more or less for granted. I shall simply assert that . . . because they are in the hands of the state, because the state exercises complete control over them, it follows that the

> *state should take responsibility for them and owes a correlative duty*
> *for their care . . . In England and Wales the prison authorities owe a*
> *common law duty of care to prisoners to take reasonable care for*
> *their safety. (Liebling, 1996: 23)*

Indeed, the view that prison personnel should take greater individual care of children, and that the prison authorities should raise general standards, has made a very significant policy impression over the last two years (*see* Chapter 4). Much of this new emphasis has focused upon improving methods of vulnerability/risk assessment to identify and screen out the most vulnerable children, but this is itself a source of some concern.

CONCERN 7: THE INHERENT RISKS OF RISK ASSESSMENT

In Chapter 1 (*see* pp. 6–8) the difficulties in defining vulnerability were discussed. It was also noted that for children being remanded into prisons vulnerability/risk assessments are frequently impeded by a lack of time and background information. Towl and Crighton (2000: 91) have observed that 'risk assessment and risk management is concerned with uncertainty. As such, it is logically impossible for any risk assessment, however good, to predict an outcome with 100 per cent accuracy'. In other words, even the most thorough and expertly executed assessments can not guarantee safety. It follows, therefore, that institutionally expedient, hasty and necessarily cursory assessments, of the type routinely applied to children in prisons, will inevitably carry serious risks. They are not meaningful safeguards and any pretence otherwise is profoundly misguided.

Indeed, there is no single profile of the child who will self-harm or attempt suicide while held on remand in prison. Some children who appear to conform to stereotypical constructions of vulnerability appear to 'cope' without incident, while others who might be expected to 'do their time' unproblematically, experience serious difficulties. While all children struggle with their experience of confinement, individual reactions to emotional pain and environmental pressure differ, making neat predictions difficult. Self-harm and suicide among the youngest prisoners is likely to be relatively impulsive and situationally-induced. Perhaps the clearest indicator of the limitations of risk/vulnerability assessments as predictive instruments lies in the fact that 70 per cent of people who commit suicide in prison are assessed as *not at risk* at the time of their death (McHugh and Snow, 2000: 21).

Despite the limitations of such assessment processes, the Prison Service and the Youth Justice Board for England and Wales have invested considerable effort into developing them and applying them more widely, as shall be discussed in Chapter 4 (*see* pp. 72–83). Given the conspicuous emphasis on risk/vulnerability assessments – especially at the point when children first arrive at prisons – it is curious that many of the children interviewed for this book did not appear to be aware that such assessment had even taken place. Equally, many prison staff were dissatisfied with the new arrangements not least because they neither had the time nor the requisite skills, experience and knowledge to administer them to the standards they thought necessary. For the children and the staff such risk/vulnerability assessments suited the purposes of institutional interest more effectively than the imperatives of child-prisoner care (*see* pp. 134–140). Ultimately, the prison is not a caring environment, and prison officers, irrespective of their personal commitment, are not equipped or resourced to provide the tailored professional care that children require. No amount of risk/vulnerability assessment will alter that stark truth.

CONCERN 8: CARING FOR CHILDREN IN PRISON – AN IMPOSSIBLE TASK?

> *Young prisoners often need more of everything. They need more one to one attention, more supervision, more contact with staff, more contact with each other, more protection from themselves and other people, more challenging, more reassurance, more understanding and more forgiveness.*
>
> (Her Majesty's Chief Inspector of Prisons, 1997: 63)

> *In recent years the massively increased numbers of children sent to custody have been dumped on prison service establishments, in a prison system that has not, traditionally, recognised that it has a role in caring for children in need of care, development and*

control. Within this system children are, quite frankly, lost.

(Her Majesty's Chief Inspector of Prisons, 1997: 63)

The juxtaposition of these statements is telling. The vulnerabilities and care needs of child remand prisoners are well-established but the prison system is singularly ill-equipped to meet them. During the research for this book I met many fine staff in prisons who were committed – often against all the odds – to working with children. I met other staff who were more equivocal in this respect (*see* pp. 140–151). However, despite the best efforts of those staff who care, it is apparent that providing for the needs of children in prison is a difficult, if not impossible, task for three primary reasons.

First, the question of values, roles and responsibilities and their tensions and contradictions. The primary role of the prison officer is to maintain discipline, order and institutional security. Set against this is the duty of care, which arguably becomes more sharply focused when the prisoner is also a child. This incongruous duality of controlling and caring roles is the inevitable source of conceptual ambiguity and operational difficulty, especially in Personal Officer Schemes. Such schemes – whereby a named officer is allocated particular responsibility for a child/children – often apply to juvenile remand prisoners:

There were difficulties in the operation of Personal Officer Schemes for remand prisoners where the turnover was higher than for sentenced prisoners and there were no clear guidelines as to how officers were intended to meet the requirements of the role. Staff told us that they had insufficient time to give personal attention to prisoners, and had no common understanding of how far they were expected to go in caring for them . . . They understood that if a prisoner approached them, they should be helpful and advise the prisoner how to receive help, but most did not see it as their responsibility to approach prisoners to check on their well-being and make notes on their records. Some staff believed that this would undermine their role as supervisors, controllers and enforcers of discipline.

(Her Majesty's Chief Inspector of Prisons, 2000: 111)

The sense that the personal officer role is essentially conceived as a passive/reactive function, as distinct from a pro-active child-centred responsibility, is confirmed in an analysis of seven Young Offender Institutions, where children who had been allocated Personal Officers were asked how regularly their nominated Officer came to find them. The children's responses give little indication of positive care with 48 per cent of those children consulted in the 'best' institution giving 'never at all' answers, compared to 89 per cent of those in the 'worst' (Her Majesty's Chief Inspector of Prisons, 2001: 49).

Second is the question of resources and staffing levels. Her Majesty's Chief Inspector of Prisons (1997: 31) has commented upon 'staffing levels which are wholly inadequate if children . . . are to receive the individual attention they need'. During interviews with prison officers I was frequently told of the pressures imposed by insufficient staffing and extraordinarily high staff-juvenile remand prisoner ratios.

Third is the question of staff training. To meet the compelling needs of children within the harsh environment of prison, staff need developed knowledge, skills and ongoing training. Again, and in spite of the best efforts of many staff, this is simply not the case in practice. Prison officers *very* rarely have any specific education, training and/or experience in meeting the needs of distressed, disadvantaged and sometimes difficult children when they are appointed, and this is unlikely to be rectified once they are in post. Indeed, Her Majesty's Chief Inspector of Prisons (1997: 66) has observed that 'currently there is very little specific training in working with young people given to Prison Officer recruits', and although the Chief Inspector has acknowledged some recent improvement in this area, he continues to be 'concerned' about the 'need to improve the training given to all those working with juveniles' (Her Majesty's Chief Inspector of Prisons, 2001: 26). Providing an appropriate service to children in prison that recognises their collective and individual needs, is extraordinarily complex. The bottom line, as the Howard League (1995: 67) has noted, is that staff 'are asked to do a job they are neither trained nor equipped to do' (*see also* Howard League, 2001 and 2001a).

CHAPTER *4*

The reform of the juvenile secure estate

THE YOUTH JUSTICE BOARD AND NEW ARRANGEMENTS FOR THE MANAGEMENT OF SECURE AND PENAL SETTINGS

The Crime and Disorder Act 1998 provided for the establishment of a new executive non-departmental public body – the Youth Justice Board for England and Wales. The principal responsibilities of the Board include advising the Home Secretary on the operation of the youth justice system, monitoring performance, establishing standards and supporting new practice initiatives. No sooner had the Board been established when it turned its attention to the question of youth custody, advising the Home Secretary that 'there is clear evidence that the current arrangements for juvenile secure facilities are highly unsatisfactory' (Youth Justice Board, 1998: 12). In many respects the Youth Justice Board was simply amplifying an earlier message from the Home Office comprehensive spending review of secure and penal facilities for children, which had:

... little positive to say about the present arrangements for ... remanded and sentenced children and young people. Regime standards are inconsistent and often poor. **Costs** vary considerably. There is no effective oversight or long-term **planning** for juvenile secure accommodation as a whole. In practice there is no definable juvenile secure estate ... fundamental change is needed to the way *in which the secure estate is **planned** and **managed** if it is to meet the aim of providing accommodation and regimes appropriate to the age and maturity of the young people held in custody on remand or under sentence and which addresses their offending behaviour and wider developmental needs.*

(Summary of the Government's response to the Home Office Comprehensive Spending Review of Secure Accommodation for remanded and sentenced juveniles, July 1998 – cited in Youth Justice Board, 1998: 14, my emphasis)

Furthermore, such observations echoed authoritative findings from the Department of Health's Children's Safeguards Review (Utting, 1997) and Her Majesty's Chief Inspector of Prisons (1997), both of which raised serious concerns about the conditions and treatment endured by children in prison. With such weight of evidence behind it, the Youth Justice Board confidently proclaimed that:

*. . . substantial changes need to be made to the **management** of juvenile secure facilities, including the secure units run by local authorities, young offender institutions and remand centres run by the prison agency, the existing and commissioned secure training centres and the Youth Treatment Centre run by the Department of Health. (Youth Justice Board, 1998: 14, my emphasis)*

Indeed, the root-and-branch reform advocated by the Board was very well received at Government level, but two points of qualification should be made here.

First, although the Board's initial emphasis was limited to the *youth justice system*, the 'substantial changes' that were proposed – and subsequently implemented – impacted across the *full range* of secure provision. This is very significant and the Youth Justice Board reforms have arguably had a negative effect on secure facilities accommodating children placed under civil statute (*see* below and pp. 119–122).

Second, even if 'it would not be true to say that all concern with the welfare of children and young people in trouble has disappeared' (Smith, 1999: 149), it certainly *is* the case that contemporary policy and practice developments in youth justice have emphasised correctional responses underpinned by managerial efficiency (Goldson, 1999b and 2000; Muncie, 1999; Pitts, 2001). This general emphasis has applied more specifically to reforming the system of secure and penal settings for children. The focus has essentially rested with the efficiency of correctional processes as distinct from intrinsic child welfare concerns. Thus the primary objective has been to make the expanded system of locked institutions 'work better', rather than to question the fundamental practice of locking up children and the very legitimacy of the institutions themselves (Goldson and Peters, 2000).

Within this context it is not inconsistent to insist that institutional regimes must be based upon 'clear principles', that there 'should be a structured and caring environment' and that such places 'should be safe and secure' (Youth Justice Board, 1998: 3), providing that the overall priorities of managerial rationality (efficiency, economy and effectiveness) go undisturbed. It follows then, that the establishments in the newly reconfigured juvenile secure estate have had centrally-determined 'standards' imposed upon them; are classified as 'authorised' or 'accredited'; must operate and 'deliver' in accordance with 'contracting conditions'; and are expected to provide 'placements' that are then 'purchased' or 'commissioned' (Youth Justice Board, 1998). In the final analysis, the practice and language of commerce and business has been introduced whereby 'supply' meets 'demand' with 'efficiency' and 'effectiveness' within the 'affordable market place' of child incarceration. Such managerial processes may serve to 'drive up standards' and 'improve performance' as is claimed by the Youth Justice Board (2001), with possible benefits for children held in secure and penal settings (although the evidence below and through Chapters 5 and 6 would suggest that such claims – if at all valid – are at least subject to qualification). The central issue, however, is that the very same processes occur *without* any questioning of the actual practice of locking up children, and *within* a context which suggests that such practice serves deterrent, correctional and/or rehabilitative purposes – for which there is little if any evidence (Goldson, 2001a; Goldson and Peters, 2000).

THE JUVENILE SECURE ESTATE

THE ROLE OF THE YOUTH JUSTICE BOARD
The Youth Justice Board assumed primary responsibility for
planning, contracting, commissioning and purchasing placements
within the re-configured juvenile secure estate in April 2000.
Alongside this, the Board also defines the operational standards for
the composite institutions within the estate, and monitors
performance.

INSTITUTIONAL CAPACITY
The juvenile secure estate is an amalgam of three sectors, which
together provide the capacity for locking up children:
* thirteen Young Offender Institutions (YOIs), which are the
  responsibility of the Prison Service
* thirty Local Authority Secure Units (LASUs), which are managed
  by Social Services Departments under the national aegis of the
  Department of Health
* three Secure Training Centres (STCs), which are provided by the
  private sector (Youth Justice Board, 2001a: 14).

In 2000/01 the three sectors provided the youth justice system with a
total of 3250 places, mostly within the Prison Service.

STANDARDS, CONTRACTS AND INSPECTION
The notion of improving the performance of secure and penal
institutions by imposing standards, establishing contractual
arrangements and scrutinising levels of compliance through
inspection and monitoring pre-dates the formation of the Youth
Justice Board. Her Majesty's Chief Inspector of Prisons (1997: 75)
had earlier recommended that 'authorities responsible for the custody
of children should be obliged to fulfill detailed specifications which
should be the subject of contracts. These should reflect clear
principles applicable to that age group and be closely monitored to
ensure compliance'. In many respects the Youth Justice Board has
worked to realise this recommendation and it recently reported that it
'has operated a consultative but robust relationship with its providers

since April 2000, concentrating on driving up standards and transforming regimes' (Youth Justice Board, 2001: 14). The Board has not only issued generic *National Standards for Youth Justice* (Youth Justice Board, 2000) but it has:

• established a partnership agreement with the Prison Service run through 'Service Delivery Agreements' with each of the 13 Young Offender Institutions within the 'under 18 estate' (Hughes and Thompson, 2000)

• settled arrangements with the Home Office to manage existing Secure Training Centre contracts

• issued a 'Generic Service Specification' for 'Local Authority Juvenile Secure Accommodation' together with a 'Service Credit Scheme' tailored to each individual unit

• attached 'Compliance Monitors' to each of the contracted establishments who, in turn, report to 'Compliance Managers' with regard to service performance.

COMMISSIONING SUPPLY AND FORECASTING DEMAND

In order to fulfill its commissioning functions and run its contracting arrangements, the Youth Justice Board – in consultation with the Home Office and the Department of Health – has established purchasing agreements with the above placement providers, based upon agreed costings and service specifications. This process requires an awareness of the likely demand for placements in secure and penal settings for children. Predicting demand, without having control of all of the determining variables, is an extraordinarily complex (not to mention risky) exercise as the Board had earlier anticipated:

> . . . there remain formidable problems of forecasting the demand for places in juvenile secure facilities and matching supply of places to demand . . . Within a discrete juvenile secure estate it will be very important to have an accurate forecast of the future demand for places . . . broadly speaking the right amount of places must be in place to cope with court decisions. At the present time there is considerable uncertainty in this area . . .
>
> (Youth Justice Board, 1998: 32–33)

The Board was equally aware of the consequences of under-estimating demand, particularly in respect of placing children in the most appropriate institutions:

> *Projections varying from 2500 to 4200 places are simply too wide for sensible planning . . . These figures are crude estimates and need further refinement but they suggest that there may well be* **very little space** *. . . This would have the effect of **removing flexibility** from the system as a whole and **preventing young people being placed according to their need.***
>
> *(Youth Justice Board, 1998: 34–37, my emphasis)*

As the Youth Justice Board has been keen to emphasise progressive change and improved standards with the juvenile secure estate, and the Government has been equally keen to maintain its 'tough' position on youth crime by providing the Courts with extended powers to lock up children, it is not surprising that the demand for placements has continued to impose pressure on the supply side. Moreover, the consequences of excessive demand are clear, and despite the best-intentioned efforts of all involved, the inappropriate placement of vulnerable children (within prisons – the sector comprising the bulk of supply) will always be a real possibility (*see* below and pp. 83–85).

PLACEMENTS AND THE QUESTION OF VULNERABILITY

As noted above, the managerial efficiency of the juvenile secure estate has comprised the primary thrust of the reform agenda, and the stated determination to 'humanise' the practice of locking up children is found within this wider context. In order to achieve this latter goal a systematic approach to placements has been introduced. Indeed, in its early advice to the Home Secretary, the Youth Justice Board identified a number of principles that would inform the placement of children within the juvenile secure estate:

> *. . . young people should be placed in accommodation, which* **most effectively meets their needs** *and the risk of harm that they pose to themselves and others. The accommodation should be appropriate for their age, emotional maturity and* **level of**

*vulnerability . . . placements for remanded and sentenced juveniles should be based on a **comprehensive assessment** of their needs and risks completed to defined national standards . . . juveniles should be accommodated as close to their home community as possible . . . those on **remand** . . . have **particular needs** as a result of the anxieties and uncertainties of being held on remand for which they may require **considerable support.***

(Youth Justice Board, 1998: 26–27, my emphasis)

This provides for a tidy rationality within which the placement process takes account of children's specific vulnerabilities and matches them – on the basis of 'comprehensive assessment' – with the most appropriate institution within the estate. Furthermore, special attention is afforded to children on remand in recognition of their 'particular needs'.

In order to run this process the Youth Justice Board has established a centralised national Placements Team, which takes the strategic overview of the contracted placements within the juvenile secure estate and – in conjunction with the locally based Youth Offending Teams – allocates places accordingly. However, as noted earlier, the intrinsic tensions of the supply-demand relation, together with the competing interests of different constituencies of children, complicate the placement process. Given that the overwhelming majority of available places are located within the Prison Service sector, it is inevitable that such tensions and complications will be most evident in the pressing demand for placements in secure accommodation. Moreover, the law (quite correctly) not only precludes the placement of all children under the age of 15 in prison custody, but it also severely limits the similar placement of 15- to 17-year-old girls. Thus the determinations of statute mean that these constituencies of children have 'first call' on the places within Secure Training Centres and/or secure accommodation. This reduces the options available to the Youth Justice Board's Placement Team, leaving 15- to 16-year-old boys (irrespective of their needs and vulnerabilities) to face the distinct probability of a prison sector placement, and exposing 17-year-old boys to the virtual certainty of the same. Furthermore, as noted in Chapter 3 (*see* pp. 43–44), the implementation of Section 130 of the Criminal Justice and Police Act 2001 will serve to further reduce room for manoeuvre in this respect, effectively condemning *all* remanded 15- and 16-year-old boys to prison.

As was also discussed in Chapter 3 (*see* pp. 41 and 44), however, Section 98 of the Crime and Disorder Act 1998 provides limited legal safeguards for such boys if they are judged to be vulnerable *and* a place is available in secure accommodation (otherwise they go to prison). Thus the 'comprehensive assessment' to which the Youth Justice Board refers is now critically important for such children.

'JOINED-UP' ASSESSMENT

The Youth Justice Board has emphasised the importance of a continuous or 'joined-up' process of assessment, starting at the pre-court stage and progressing into the institution itself:

> When young people are about to enter [the juvenile secure estate] there should be a rigorous, comprehensive and standard assessment of their . . . needs . . . This work should start when a YOT member identifies a need to find a placement and should continue in the institution. (Youth Justice Board, 1998: 17–18)

The processes of assessing the vulnerability of children on remand are particularly relevant here. The *overall* assessment process involves contributions from various agencies and, in its complete joined-up form, it comprises six discrete but inter-connected stages, each accompanied by specific documentation.

ASSESSMENT STAGE ONE: ASSET

> A past failing of youth justice has been the absence of **systematic assessment** of young offenders . . . during last year the Board has worked with Oxford University and several YOTs to produce **a standard assessment tool** for use with young offenders – ASSET. From April 2000 YOTs are using ASSET to assess **each young offender**. (Youth Justice Board, 2000a: 3, my emphasis)

ASSET is used by the YOT to determine why a young person has offended, what their family and lifestyle circumstances are, whether they have specific mental health or drug and alcohol-related problems, if they attend school and **what level of risk they pose** *to others and* **to themselves***.*

(Youth Justice Board, 2001a: 7, my emphasis)

ASSET is a detailed form that should be completed for *each child* and *all children* who come into contact with the youth justice system. The form has a dual purpose: it is designed to assess the risk that child offenders might pose to others, and it is also intended to assess the child's vulnerability or, more specifically, the risk that they present to themselves. Vulnerability is narrowly viewed here in terms of the risk of self-harm and/or suicide (*see* pp. 7–8).

For children at the pre-court stage, a shorter version of ASSET – the ASSET Bail Assessment Profile – has to be completed and this also has a dual assessment function. Bail ASSET addresses the child's offending, bail and remand history and, in so doing, is designed to inform an assessment of the child's risk to others, but it also covers critical issues of the child's personal and social circumstances, which might be indicative of vulnerability. In particular, Bail ASSET requires the assessor to consider 'foreseeable events or circumstances likely to cause him/her significant distress or difficulties'; 'the young person's ability to cope with the difficulties'; 'any previous incidents of self-harm'; and any earlier 'suicide attempts' particularly 'self-harm or suicide incidents [which have] occurred in prison or other secure settings' (Youth Justice Board, 2000b: 3). Moreover, as discussed in Chapter 3 (*see* p. 44), Section 98 of the Crime and Disorder Act 1998 provides that in cases where the child is a 15- or 16-year old boy, and is likely to be denied bail and remanded to a penal setting, the assessment should take especial account of 'physical immaturity', 'emotional immaturity' and 'propensity to self-harm' (*ibid*: 4).

The practical processes within which ASSET assessments are found are defined by *National Standards*. Standard 3 applies to assessment *per se* and this is accompanied by Standard 6, which focuses more closely on court work and remands. The Standards are

unequivocal on the question of vulnerability and penal remands for
15- and 16-year olds:

> *The court, if considering remanding a young offender to secure*
> *facilities, should request that the YOT makes an assessment . . .*
> *the YOT Manager must ensure a vulnerability assessment is done*
> *by a YOT member trained in the use of ASSET on all 15 and 16 year*
> *olds whom the court is considering remanding to secure facilities*
> *. . . a YOT member must interview all young offenders who have*
> *been remanded to secure facilities before they leave the court . . .*
> *to assess whether there is an enhanced risk of suicide or self-harm*
> *. . . The manager of the secure facility must ensure the offender's*
> *needs and level of vulnerability are assessed in the light of*
> *information provided by the YOT.*
>
> *(Youth Justice Board, 2000: paras 6.4.1, 6.5.1, 6.6.2 and 6.7.5)*

Here, therefore, the joined-up nature of assessment is such that the
Bail ASSET form is meant to travel with the child to the penal setting
to alert prison personnel to any perceived vulnerabilities at the point
of reception. The Youth Justice Board has reported that this function
of ASSET has been warmly received by YOT staff and prison
personnel alike. The Board quotes a YOT manager reasoning:

> *I think the best uses of ASSET are in the relationship between the*
> *YOT and the secure estate. The ASSET can help identify a*
> *vulnerable child and better safeguard their welfare. Of course,*
> *assessment is not a science and it is impossible to predict exactly*
> *how everyone will behave, but the part of ASSET that refers to the*
> *possibility of self-harm is extremely helpful for secure staff when*
> *they are admitting a young person.*

A casework manager from a Young Offenders Institution reflects:

> *I think ASSET is a brilliant aid to us when a young man comes into*
> *reception . . . [it is] particularly important to a young person coming*
> *into custody for the first time. (Youth Justice Board, 2001b: 3)*

However, the manager from the YOI also adds significantly:

> *On an average day we can expect 20 remands . . . often there is*
> *only one case worker on duty, so even with only fifteen pages to*

read through that is still a difficult task to complete . . . to prevent vital information being overlooked. The other area that needs improvement is making sure that the ASSET form actually reaches us from court. (ibid: 3)

This final comment identifies two crucial issues: first, the pressure and volume of work that routinely confronts YOI staff at the point of reception; and second, the extent to which ASSET documentation – despite National Standards – does not reach the YOI at the same time as the child remand prisoner. These issues will be examined in greater detail below and in Chapter 6 (*see* pp. 134–140).

ASSESSMENT STAGE TWO: THE REMAND WARRANT

In cases where a child is remanded to prison, the Magistrates' Courts Act 1980 and Statutory Instrument Number 2071 – the Magistrates' Courts (Children and Young Persons) Rules 1992 – requires the court to record in a warrant the child's name, address and date of birth, together with details of the alleged offence and the court's action (including the duration of the remand). A Young Offender Institution will not admit a child without receiving such a warrant. The remand warrant should also be accompanied by a bail form carrying an explanation as to why bail has been refused in accordance with the Bail Act 1976.

Information regarding the alleged offence and the reason for refusal of bail is crucial in assisting prison personnel to assess the vulnerability of the child. Moreover, Section 29(1) of Statutory Instrument Number 2071 – the Magistrates' Courts (Children and Young Persons) Rules 1992 – also provides that 'forms may be used with such variation as the circumstances may require' and so best practice would involve attaching additional documentation (in appropriate cases) relating to the child's perceived vulnerability.

ASSESSMENT STAGE THREE: THE POST-COURT REPORT (PCR)

The PCR is a four-page document in duplicate, designed to provide '*essential information* for custodial facilities, to be completed by YOT staff for *all* children and young people *remanded* or sentenced to custody' (Youth Justice Board, 2000: 1, my emphasis).

For children remanded into penal custody the PCR requires the YOT worker to include information on the child's personal and family details; any special communication needs the child may have; the child's health status, including treatment that may be urgently required for substance misuse; the risk of harm that the child may pose to others; the child's vulnerability; and relevant additional information. Clearly, the PCR is an important document, which should be completed in respect of *every* remanded child at *each* separate court appearance. The PCR is particularly important for a child's first remand and it should accompany each and every other document referred to in this section in order to provide a comprehensive and joined-up assessment. However, this does not appear to be happening in practice as is discussed in more detail below.

ASSESSMENT STAGE FOUR: THE PRISONER ESCORT RECORD (PER)

Arrangements for the transport of remanded children from court to prison are ultimately the responsibility of Prisoner Escort and Custody Services (PECS). In turn, at the regional level, services to transfer children from court to custody have been privatised and PECS has let contracts to independent escort operators who then serve as the direct providers of the service.

Prisoner escorts are meant to complete a PER form for every child they transfer from court to custody. The form requires the escort to assess the child's risk (either to self or others) and three 'tick-box' columns entitled 'medical', 'security' and 'other' identify a range of 'risk categories'. The 'other' column includes 'drugs/alcohol issues', 'suicide/self-harm' and 'vulnerability'. The PER also obliges the escort to keep a 'record of events' during transit. In addition to the PER the escort also has a 'Prisoner Warning Notice' at their disposal to record any additional information relating to the child's 'possible risk of self-harm or suicide'. A number of issues were raised during interviews with children and prison personnel in relation to escort arrangements in general, and the PER in particular, and these are discussed in Chapter 6 (*see* pp. 132–134).

ASSESSMENT STAGE FIVE: ARRIVAL AT THE PRISON: THE
RECEPTION INTERVIEW AND THE T1:V FORM

National Standards provide that:

> Secure facility staff must undertake a reception interview within **one
> hour** of the offender's arrival that assesses the offender's **needs**
> and **level of vulnerability**. Staff undertaking the interview must see
> **written information** about the offender that will have **already been
> sent to the secure facility**.
>
> (Youth Justice Board, 2000: para 8.1.2, my emphasis)

This standard emphasises both the importance of the reception
interview, and the necessity for 'written information' to accompany
the arrival of the child at the prison in order to establish the child's
'needs' and 'level of vulnerability'. For the purposes of structuring
the reception interview and systematically recording information, the
T1:V form was implemented in each of the 13 YOIs holding juvenile
remand and sentenced prisoners in April 2001. Prison reception
personnel are advised:

> The T1:V form is part of a **set of . . . documentation**. Together these
> provide a system for ensuring that **essential information** about
> young people in custody is noted and communicated clearly . . . to
> provide appropriate care and supervision . . . Its purpose is to help
> staff undertaking the reception interview to **assess the young
> person's vulnerability** . . . and to make plans to minimise the risk of
> the young person harming themselves . . . while they are in custody.
> Vulnerability is susceptibility to significant physical or emotional
> harm and distress. Clear, accurate and **shared assessments** of the
> risk of harm will be successful in identifying ways to reduce the
> likelihood of such harm occurring.
>
> (Youth Justice Board, 2001c: 1, my emphasis)

The T1:V form is a detailed document that necessarily raises
complex and deeply sensitive personal issues with children within an
hour of their arrival at the prison. Indeed, the YOI reception officer is
required to discuss histories of self-harm; mental and physical health;
anxieties induced by prison detention; bereavement; parental
separation; family breakdown; the impact of severed significant

relationships; victimisation and bullying, and (alleged) offence details with the child in order to construct a 'risk management plan'. Moreover, such prison personnel are rather starkly advised:

> *Do not leave any section blank. Either the 'yes' or the 'no' box should be ticked every time they appear. (ibid)*

Equally, such staff are advised:

> *Always read the PCR form and the YOT's ASSET assessment before starting the initial assessment. (ibid)*

This latter point assumes that the joined-up assessment objective is being followed in practice and that such documentation is readily available at YOI reception. Moreover, the detailed and sensitive nature of the issues raised by the T1:V form apparently assumes that honed skills, ample time and an appropriate confidential environment is available in order to facilitate the interview. However, as discussed below and in Chapter 6 (*see* pp. 134–140), neither assumption is confirmed by the evidence, which places a serious question mark against the efficacy of the new joined-up assessment arrangements.

ASSESSMENT STAGE SIX: FIRST RECEPTION HEALTH SCREEN

As well as the reception interview and the completion of the T1:V documentation, a child remanded into prison custody will also be interviewed by a nurse from the YOI's Health Care staff. The nurse is required to complete a further form entitled the 'First Reception Health Screen'. This form is issued by the Prison Service and it advises the nurse to begin by explaining 'to the prisoner that the purpose of the interview is to gain a brief confidential medical and psychiatric history'. A remanded juvenile prisoner will then be taken through a sequence of questions relating to their 'physical health', any 'drug/alcohol history' and their 'mental health' before being invited to offer any 'additional information'. The questions featured within the mental health sequence are unrefined and include: 'have you ever deliberately harmed yourself?' and if so 'how and why?'; have you ever attempted suicide?' and if so 'method tried'; 'has any close relative or friend ever attempted suicide?'; 'do you feel like hurting yourself at the moment?' and 'are you feeling suicidal?'.

SUMMARY

The reform of the juvenile secure estate has not been limited to macro-level infra-structural change. Indeed, the reform agenda has cut deep into micro-level practice, and the notion of joined-up assessment is an expression of this. The Youth Justice Board has repeatedly emphasised the importance of systematic assessment to identify the most vulnerable children and to address their needs, and in certain respects this is to be welcomed. However, there are three conspicuous practical problems with this process which merit brief mention here.

First, the very concept of vulnerability is too narrowly defined (*see* p. 7). Although the Youth Justice Board (2001c: 1) has stated that 'vulnerability is susceptibility to significant physical or emotional harm and distress', in practice vulnerability is essentially code for manifest suicidal intent. Indeed, as noted in Chapter 3 (*see* pp. 50–52), there is an abundance of evidence to suggest that the overwhelming majority of children held in prisons on remand are 'susceptible to significant physical or emotional harm and distress', a point consistently raised during the interviews with both children and prison personnel (*see* pp. 127–132). The juvenile secure estate simply does not have the capacity to attend to children's routine vulnerability but instead has to focus far more sharply upon the most extreme cases. New assessment arrangements may, or may not, screen-out the most exceptionally vulnerable children but they will do little, if anything, to appease the vulnerabilities of the majority.

Second, the assessment process itself is seriously flawed and deeply problematic. Perhaps the most helpful way of illustrating this point is to map the process as it applies to child remand prisoners – for example – a 15-year-old boy facing the prospect of a prison remand. Such a child will almost certainly be produced in court having been held in police custody the night before. A YOT worker will then be required to undertake an initial assessment in order to complete the ASSET documentation (assessment stage one). Once the court has determined that bail is to be refused a remand warrant will then be completed, which may require additional assessment (assessment stage two). The child will then be returned to holding cells in the court custody area while awaiting transfer to the YOI. At this stage a YOT worker will need to complete a further assessment in accordance with the PCR requirements (assessment stage three). Several hours might pass before the escort services are ready to transfer the child to the YOI, during which time he will continue to be held in custody. Once the escort service is ready to transfer the child, he will be taken to prison in a cellular vehicle. The conditions endured by the child during transfer will be spartan (*see* pp. 132–134) and at some stage the escort will be required to complete the PER, requiring further assessment and questioning (assessment stage four). When the child arrives at the YOI he will then be exposed to two further assessments as part of the reception process: the 'T1: V' (assessment stage five) and the First Reception Health Screen (assessment stage six).

During this joined-up process the child will be interviewed by a *minimum* of five different adults (the same person might lead assessment stages one and three), none of whom will necessarily be previously known to him. Beforehand, in-between times and afterwards the same child will be locked up. Each interview will raise complex, deeply sensitive, personal and confidential issues with the child. Every episode within the overall process will almost certainly (and necessarily) be rushed and take place within entirely unsuitable conditions (with very little prospect of a congenial and relaxed setting affording privacy and confidentiality, *see* pp. 137–140). Suicide and self-harm will consistently and repeatedly be raised with the child. The formal skills of the 'assessors', together with their specialist training and qualifications, will inevitably be limited. At the end of this crude and intense process of assessment, the child will be left alone to reflect upon the day, locked in a cell with only his sense of bewilderment and confusion for company. The only distraction for the child will be the intimidating shouting and calls emanating from the barred 'window' spaces of adjacent cells (*see* pp. 144–147). The documentary expression of such an assessment process presents a humane and caring impression. The reality of the very same process could just as readily be regarded as abusive and damaging.

Third, the overall process of assessment is more disjointed than joined-up. Fragmentation is evident not only as outlined above, but it is also apparent in the documentation that eventually arrives at the YOI with the child. Despite the new assessment arrangements, there is burgeoning evidence to suggest that, in practice, the assessment process haemorrhages crucial information, leaving reception staff at YOIs with no alternative but to admit child remand prisoners with the barest of details (*see* below and pp. 134–137).

THE LIMITATIONS OF REFORM: SOME CONCERNS ABOUT THE NEW ARRANGEMENTS

The treatment of juveniles is, in general unrecognisably better than it was, following the introduction of the Youth Justice Board . . .

I now conduct inspections of every Prison Service establishment holding juveniles every three years, and with OFSTED inspectors, an educational inspection every year. I find the YJB's principles and policies both radical and exciting, and believe that they mark a very real step forward . . . but set against that . . . much remains to be done to improve the treatment and conditions of those on remand.

(Her Majesty's Chief Inspector of Prisons, 2001: 2 and 25–6)

The Youth Justice Board (2000a: 18–19) has expressed its determination to provide 'constructive custody' by 'pushing up standards'. The means by which the Board has set about this task has been reviewed above. The reform agenda has apparently produced some welcome improvement in the conditions and treatment of children in prison but a number of pressing concerns remain. Some of these concerns have been considered in Chapter 3 (*see* pp. 50–66), and the interviews with children and prison personnel (*see* Chapter 6) give lucid expression to others. However, three key concerns relating to the new juvenile secure estate arrangements merit some immediate attention.

CONCERN 1: POLICY-PRACTICE TENSIONS

The Board recommends that there should be a change in the status of prison establishments in the future. Once all juvenile secure facilities are being run on the basis of the [new] regime standards, and according to a contract of service level agreement with the Youth Justice Board . . . although run by Prison Service staff, these establishments would not be prisons. This should be reflected in a change of name. (Youth Justice Board, 1998: 24)

Prisons for children and young people are given a variety of names . . . the names are intended to show that these are not prisons, but places of good intent, where the previous bad influences of the young people's lives will be corrected by caring people.

(Stern, 1998: 157)

Through its reform agenda, the Youth Justice Board has been at pains to impress that the imprisonment of children is being systematically humanised. Indeed, the Board has gone so far to suggest that once all of the reforms are complete, prisons will not be prisons!

There are a number of problems and associated concerns with such reasoning but the focus that follows is on its practical effect, which has been to produce a substantial increase in custodial disposals for children (for a fuller discussion *see* Goldson, 2002). Indeed, as Cohen so perceptively observed almost 20 years ago, 'it is by making the system appear less harsh, that people are encouraged to use it more often' (Cohen, 1985: 98). In other words, if the courts are repeatedly presented with the message that the harmful excesses of child imprisonment are being designed-out through reform, and that standards have been pushed up to such an extent that custody serves a 'constructive' purpose, it is not surprising that they exercise their powers (to remand and sentence children to periods of prison detention) with increasing regularity.

This problem is only accentuated by the Government's associated determination to remain 'tough on crime'. Such policy resolve has been consistently expressed through its willingness to provide the courts with ever-increasing powers to detain children across the full range of secure facilities (*see* pp. 42–44). So there is a situation in which the value of custody is trumpeted, and the powers of the courts to use it are expanded. There can only be one result: 'youth prisons are near bursting' (*The Times*, 23 August 2001). Indeed, in a circular to every Youth Court and YOT in England and Wales, Norman Warner, the Chairperson of the Youth Justice Board, reported that 'the use of custody for juveniles has been rising steadily since the mid-1990s and it rose again between April 2000 and March 2001' (Warner, 2001: para 4). In particular Warner drew attention to the substantial increase in short custodial sentences being imposed upon younger children and girls. This is a major problem, and one that will be intensified by the further relaxation of remand criteria and the full implementation of Section 130 of the Criminal Justice and Police Act 2001 (*see* pp. 43–44), which '. . . will put the already overcrowded prison and youth justice systems under immense pressure as they struggle to find enough places' (Travis, 2002: 1).

The tensions between *policies* that ultimately serve to increase the use of custody for children, and *practices* that aim to take account of individual needs and vulnerabilities by way of a considered placement strategy, are apparent. Such policies exacerbate the pressures upon the juvenile secure estate and, as such, they substantially diminish its capacity to facilitate placement flexibility. Furthermore, given that there is a particularly notable increase in the use of custody for younger children and girls (who by law can only be placed in Secure Training Centres or secure accommodation), this inevitably reduces the number of spaces available in secure accommodation for particularly vulnerable 15- and 16-year-old boys. It is no surprise that by far the single most significant impediment preventing vulnerable 15- and 16-year-old remand prisoners from being placed in secure accommodation as an alternative to prison, is the shortage of beds (The Children's Society, 2001: 16). Secure accommodation is increasingly 'silting-up' with younger children serving short sentences (often for non-serious offences), leaving their older counterparts, however vulnerable, to the mercy of the prison system. Moreover, the problems associated with such policy-practice tensions are not limited to children whose liberty is restricted under criminal justice statute: they also substantially impact upon the availability of services for the other constituency of children with whom this book is concerned – those within the public care and looked-after systems.

CONCERN 2: SQUEEZING-OUT WELFARE?

As noted earlier in this chapter (*see* p. 71), the Youth Justice Board has settled contracts with local authority Secure Units as an integral part of its strategy to reform the juvenile secure estate. There are two means by which the Youth Justice Board purchases placements within secure accommodation. First, by way of *block-purchase* arrangements, underpinned by contract, which guarantee that the contracted number of placements are permanently reserved and exclusively available to the Board's Placement Centre. Second, by way of *spot-purchase* arrangements, which allow the Board to secure additional placements over and above their contracted quota. Either way, any placement in secure accommodation purchased by the Youth Justice Board is a placement no longer available to local authorities and the civil courts for the purposes of restricting the liberty of children under the provisions of the Children Act 1989 (Section 25).

Throughout the process of interviews and professional consultations (particularly with Independent Persons and Guardians *ad litem*/Children's Guardians, *see* pp. 121–122), a consistent theme emerged. The professionals expressed concern that the welfare constituency of children is being squeezed-out of secure accommodation as a result of the reconfiguration and reform of the juvenile secure estate, and the Youth Justice Board's contracting arrangements. The annual statistics collated by the Department of Health appear to provide some evidence to substantiate such concern. Indeed, at 31 March 2001 all but five of the 30 Secure Units in England and Wales had contracted with the Youth Justice Board in the way described above (Department of Health, 2001). The proportion of placements sold to the Board ranges from 13 per cent in one Secure Unit to 100 per cent in some others. Overall, of the 450 placements available, the Youth Justice Board has block-purchased 267, amounting to 59 per cent of the total capacity of secure accommodation in England and Wales (Department of Health, 2001: 8).

Of course these figures do not take account of the spot-purchasing option, which is also available to the Youth Justice Board. Indeed, although the Board will inevitably make more use of its spot-purchasing option at a time when the courts are detaining increasing numbers of children within the juvenile secure estate (as just discussed), there are no official statistics currently available to gauge this. In order to assess the regularity of spot purchasing therefore, a national survey was implemented and a questionnaire sent to each of the 30 Secure Units in England and Wales (*see* p. 6). Managers from 20 Secure Units returned the questionnaire, giving a completion rate of 67 per cent.

The Secure Unit Managers were asked how regularly placements – that would otherwise be reserved for welfare purposes – were made available to the Youth Justice Board for spot purchasing.

Table 7: Regularity with which Secure Unit welfare beds are made available to the YJB for spot purchasing

Regularity of spot purchase	Number of Secure Units	% of total questionnaire respondents
Very often	7	35%
Quite often	3	15%
Rarely	7	35%
Never	3*	15%*

* Two of these units (ten per cent), had sold *all* their beds to the YJB and so had no capacity for spot-purchasing.

From this survey, it can be seen that 35 per cent of the Secure Units which returned the completed questionnaire report to selling additional placements to the Youth Justice Board *very often*, with a further 15 per cent allowing spot purchases *quite often*.

The questionnaire also invited Secure Unit Managers to comment on the principal implications and practical consequences of Youth Justice Board contracting and spot purchasing in respect of Section 25/welfare placements for their *particular Unit*. Typical responses included:

We now have less control over admissions.

This is a secure children's home and not a youth correctional facility or prison. Spot purchasing can distort that balance.

The number of short-stay cases has increased with short DTOs having a marked effect on the number of children going through in one year which is up by approximately one third . . . The increase in short term YJB cases can have a de-stabilising effect on such children [welfare placements] who see others leaving after far shorter stays whilst they do not have any end-date for going.

The Unit is now compromised in its efforts to meet the needs of two similar yet dissimilar groups – the kids have very similar needs but dissimilar legal status by virtue of their order. There is also concern that with the YJB/Section 25 mix, with a greater emphasis on offence-focused work/security issues linked to prison regimes, welfare needs generally can be overlooked for those most in need including high risk to self, survivors of abuse, significant mental health problems. We are severely compromised.

One of the practical consequences of spot purchasing is the dilemma of maintaining an ethos suitable for welfare.

The main implication is the issues raised in managing the mix. The YJB has removed the variable facility that was always present and practiced before April 2000. Placement trends for welfare beds cannot now be responded to.

The unit is not sufficient for the needs of local children. By allowing spot purchasing it can mean that a local child with welfare needs ends up being placed miles away from their home area because we are full with children from the YJB.

In my view there is a shortage of welfare placements. We are getting more phone calls asking if we have a vacancy.

Such insights from the Secure Unit Managers not only confirm that the new contracting and purchasing arrangements are producing a diminishing 'market-share' of secure accommodation for children within the welfare constituency, but they also signal other related concerns. Contracting now means that managers and senior Secure Unit staff are less able to exert their influence over admissions, which can lead to an imbalance of children and young people within the Units. The scales are increasingly tilting towards the justice constituency and this is creating operational difficulties for Unit staff. Such staff are required to comply with the demanding specifications imposed by contract with the Youth Justice Board (including regime, security and offence-focused work) on the one hand, while addressing the complex needs of children placed for quite different purposes and maintaining an 'ethos suitable for welfare' (as one manager put it), on the other. The greater the imbalance in favour of the justice constituency, the more difficult it will inevitably be to retain the notion of the 'secure children's home'. As Youth Justice Board placement imperatives continue to impose ever-greater influence, the marginalisation of welfare priorities within secure accommodation becomes increasingly apparent.

The questionnaire also asked Secure Unit Managers to consider the principal implications and practical consequences of Youth Justice Board contracting and spot purchasing in respect of Section 25/welfare placements for *secure accommodation nationally*. Similar themes emerged and typical comments included:

Very clearly the provision for Section 25 welfare placements has vastly diminished due to the YJB contracting a very substantial portion of the local authority secure estate.

There is a serious shortfall in placements for section 25 children. We have as many as 15 enquiries whenever we have a vacancy. This is a dramatic increase since the YJB contractual arrangements came about.

Welfare beds are now not as available as previously in some geographical areas. This results in welfare placements being made a long way from the child's home area. Social Services Departments are now having to take greater risks in looking after young people due to the difficulties in accessing secure beds.

There is a shortage of welfare beds. However, it is more than this there is now the dominance of the YJB cultures in secure children's homes. Managing the mix is now much more of an issue. Who is managing secure children's homes, the Department of Health or the YJB?

Based upon long-standing experience we view the mix of young people as of primary importance in our ability to help them. To contract with the YJB removes the opportunity to manage this mix. The decision to admit or not must remain with the Unit Managers but such contracting removes that.

There is some evidence of secure remands being engineered to get places for young people. Whether this is because it is the only way that Local Authorities can get secure beds or it is seen as a cheaper means of getting a secure placement is open to speculation.

There are a lot of young women coming via the YJB who have very similar needs to the welfare cases. They are the same girls coming in just via a different route.

Concern for the future of welfare placements centres on what appears to be a move towards financial security and a business partnership with the YJB and a drift away from focusing on a welfare service to young people in crisis. With the shift in emphasis there will inevitably be a shift in attitude with fewer places available for welfare. It could well be the case that that young people requiring Secure Accommodation for what are primarily welfare needs will come into Secure Accommodation eventually as a result of their consequential behaviours via the offending route rather than in recognition of need and welfare.

It's very seductive. It's lucrative. It's fixed income. It answers all your income problems and in some ways it's very attractive for units which have to run themselves as small businesses.

Again, the managers not only emphasise reduced availability of Secure Unit beds for welfare cases – together with their associated concerns as outlined above – but they also raise four additional issues.

First is the question of placement proximity to the child's home area. With fewer welfare placements, some managers are concerned that children will simply be placed wherever there is a vacancy. This will mean that some children will be placed at a considerable distance from their families, friends and home-communities, making visits difficult, and probably undermining 'care plans'. This is a problem in all areas but particularly severe in Wales, where there is only one Secure Unit:

*At present the only provision in Wales is located at the All Wales Secure Unit in Neath, South Wales. The Youth Justice Board have purchased 14 of the available 18 beds at the unit. These beds are not necessarily ring fenced for young people from Wales, and so we are still experiencing secure placements in distant locations like Durham, Exeter and Cheshire. It is also clear that the purchase agreement with the Board is **limiting the availability of local provision for welfare cases**.*

(Nacro Cymru, 2000a: 3, my emphasis)

Second is the problem of increasing risk and compounding children's vulnerability. Some managers expressed concerns that the shortage of welfare placements means that Social Services Departments will have to look after children (who would otherwise be in secure accommodation) in open placements. The same managers felt that this will inevitably fail to meet children's needs and will intensify their vulnerabilities by exposing them to increased levels of risk in the community.

Third is the question of 'pragmatic criminalisation'. A number of managers suggested that if the welfare route to secure accommodation is obstructed, some placing authorities will be inclined to explore the justice route in respect of the same children. This clearly provides a pragmatic solution to meeting the perceived needs of the child, but is deeply problematic and ethically bankrupt: it amounts to the criminalisation of the child in order to address their manifest welfare needs.

Fourth is the issue of the commercialisation of secure accommodation. As the language, practice and conventions of business are steadily imposed upon the management of secure accommodation, professionalism and the intrinsic needs of children are potentially over-shadowed and compromised by business interests. A number of managers referred to the contracting arrangements with the Youth Justice Board as 'good business'. Moreover, there is a developing perception that the clearly defined specifications of Youth Justice Board contracts, necessitating highly structured regimes and practices, are easier to manage than the more flexible child-centred approach, arguably more conducive to meeting the welfare needs of children. The combination of guaranteed income and, therefore, less problematic operational practices means that the justice constituency is a more attractive business proposition than its welfare counterpart.

These issues, and others, are further explored throughout Chapter 5.

CONCERN 3: DISJOINTED ASSESSMENT AND INFORMATION BREAKDOWN

Returning to the justice constituency of children, the processes of vulnerability and other assessments have been discussed in detail earlier in this chapter (*see* pp. 74–83). Some of the problems associated with such processes have also been considered, including information breakdown, whereby crucial documentation is lost and fails to accompany the child's arrival at the prison. This warrants further attention.

In a circular to all YOT Managers, Local Authority Secure Unit Managers, YOI Governors and Secure Training Centre Managers, the Youth Justice Board has reported that:

> It is still the case that young people are continuing to arrive at facilities with inadequate paperwork. Again this is **particularly true of prison service placements**. The relevant paperwork (Asset . . . post-court report) must be conveyed to the receiving unit with the young person, or by fax. We will be monitoring these matters and giving feedback to relevant YOTs.
>
> *(Youth Justice Board, 2000c: para 8, my emphasis)*

The Youth Justice Board does not define the extent of such poor practice but, despite its circular (and the requirements of National Standards discussed earlier, pp. 75–76), there appears to have been little improvement. Indeed, throughout the course of interviews with prison personnel (*see* pp. 134–137), a common complaint was that staff continue to work from the scantiest information on the backgrounds and vulnerabilities of children in their charge. To examine the extent of disjointed assessment and information breakdown, an audit of ASSET and Post-Court Report documentation was implemented in one YOI over a six-month period in 2001 (*see* p. 6). The audit of assessment documentation related to *every child remand prisoner* (on first arrival at the YOI) within the six-month period.

From the figures in Table 8, the information breakdown effect is apparent:

• Only 203 PCRs were received in respect of 298 children (68 per cent of the total), that is, 95 PCR's (32 per cent of the total) were 'lost' between the court and the YOI.

• A substantially worse rate of haemorrhage is evident in relation to ASSET documentation. Here, the YOI only received 108 ASSET forms (or Bail ASSET forms) for the 298 child remand prisoners (that is, 36 per cent of the total). This represents a 64 per cent haemorrhage rate.

Table 8: Juvenile remand prisoners, Post-Court Reports (PCRs) and ASSET documentation received in one YOI, Feb–July 2001

	Feb	March	April	May	June	July	Totals
Juvenile remands received[1]	53	41	40	53	61	50	**298**
PCRs received	34 (64%)	25 (61%)	28 (70%)	38 (72%)	46 (75%)	32 (64%)	**203 (68%)**
ASSETs received[2]	14 (26%)	14 (34%)	15 (38%)	24 (45%)	24 (39%)	17 (34%)	**108 (36%)**
Both PCR and ASSET received	13 (26%)	9 (22%)	9 (22%)	16 (30%)	22 (36%)	13 (26%)	**82 (28%)**
Neither PCR nor ASSET received	15 (28%)	8 (20%)	6 (15%)	7 (13%)	10 (16%)	12 (24%)	**58 (19%)**

[1] First remand and initial arrival at the YOI.
[2] Bail ASSET and/or full ASSET.

- Although, in accordance with National Standards, the YOI should receive a PCR *and* an ASSET form (the Bail version or the full ASSET document) in respect of *every* juvenile remand prisoner, this occurred in only 28 per cent of cases during the audit period.
- For 58 children (19 per cent of the total), the YOI received *neither* a PCR *nor* an ASSET (in any form). This essentially means that YOI reception staff had no substantive information for one in five child remand prisoners.

Bearing in mind the range of points that have been raised on the inevitable limitations of YOI reception assessments, and the particular vulnerabilities of child remand prisoners, the extent of information breakdown is worrying. Moreover, throughout the course of interviews with YOI personnel, officers frequently complained that even when the various forms are received, they are invariably incomplete and/or contain significant information gaps.

Despite the reform effort, the vulnerabilities of children held on remand in prisons are manifest and this central issue will be explored further in Chapter 6.

CHAPTER 5

Children, vulnerability and secure accommodation

SECURE ACCOMMODATION FROM THE INSIDE

It has already been seen how secure accommodation occupies the ambiguous conceptual space that separates the child welfare and youth justice systems. Moreover, in its welfare application, secure accommodation is a contentious resource. The practice of locking up children in order to 'protect' and 'look after' them inevitably raises complex questions for policy and practice, which are fraught with tension, dissent and discomfort. By drawing on a wide range of documentary sources and research evidence, Chapter 2 examined and analysed a number of key concerns in this respect. Similarly, the findings from the national questionnaire survey, set out in Chapter 4, introduced additional concerns with specific regard to the re-configuration of the juvenile secure estate and its principal implications for children placed in secure accommodation under civil/welfare statute. This chapter further illuminates the complexities and controversies of incarcerative child-care by reaching into the Secure Units themselves, and by providing an analytical account of the qualitative research findings drawn from in-depth interviews and consultations with children, Secure Unit staff and allied professionals.

Fifteen children, from six Secure Units in England, were interviewed, comprising approximately 23 per cent of the *total* number of children placed in secure accommodation under civil/ welfare statute in England and Wales (*see* Table 2, p. 21).

Furthermore, 20 secure accommodation staff (including senior managers, operational managers and residential social workers) were interviewed, together with 16 Independent Persons and Guardians *ad litem*/Children's Guardians involved in the placement of children in secure accommodation under civil/welfare statute, and/or with the review of their cases.

VULNERABLE CHILDREN

Children placed in secure accommodation under civil/welfare statute invariably have life-histories scarred by poverty, family breakdown and separation, public care, adult abuse and emotional trauma (Gabbidon and Goldson, 1997; Goldson, 1995; O'Neill, 2001). Indeed, the Secure Unit staff confirmed this during interview. The staff were invited to describe the typical circumstances and background characteristics of such children and their responses were depressingly consistent and included:

Ninety-nine per cent of the young people I meet have had virtually no adult guidance and support. In all of my experience there are very few young people who are 'bad'. They are mostly kids who have experienced the most appalling life experiences. It is very difficult to describe the environments that these kids come from.

(Secure Unit Deputy Manager)

Broken homes, abused by parents and family, poor and disadvantaged, deprived upbringing, never been to school. To be honest nobody gives a toss about them. Very few get visited regularly from parents and they've been in care for the best part of their lives. There is a girl in here now, she's just 14 and she has had 53 different placements. (Secure Unit Residential Social Worker)

Girls involved in child prostitution. We know they are the victims and it's the men who should be locked up but we also know that things get worse unless there is an intervention and in order to address these issues they have to be in a safe environment. It can literally be a question of life and death. For the girls who self-harm it can seem to a lay person absurd to lock them up but you have to keep them safe. (Secure Unit Manager)

There are always exceptions but generally we get young people from disadvantaged backgrounds with no significant adult in their lives with usually a background of residential care or numerous foster placements. Local authorities are quicker to secure girls and young women and you still see that bloody word 'promiscuous' on referral forms – you never see that for boys. Boys tend to do a lot more before anything is mooted on Section 25 – they normally go down the criminal route. (Secure Unit Team Leader)

Such children are routinely exposed to innumerable forms of professional intervention, counselling, assessment, case conferences and review meetings, during which their personal histories – with all of the associated pain – are continuously examined and re-examined. Therefore, the interviews with children for this research deliberately avoided any sustained and detailed focus on their individual biographies. The children were, however, invited to provide some *basic* background information, and the aggregated social profiles which emerged are very revealing:

- The sample comprised 12 girls (80 per cent) and three boys (20 per cent).
- One child was aged 12 years (7 per cent), one was aged 13 (7 per cent), seven were aged 14 (47 per cent), four were aged 15 (27 per cent), and two were aged 16 (13 per cent).
- All the children were living away from home and being looked after by Social Services Authorities and each had an allocated social worker at the time of admission to secure accommodation. Eleven (73 per cent) had been living in residential care (children's homes), three (20 per cent) were living with substitute families (foster carers) and one (7 per cent) was living at a residential school, before their admission.
- Eleven children (73 per cent) reported receiving no education at the time of admission to secure accommodation (seven of them had been excluded from school and four were not attending). Of the remaining four children, three (20 per cent) were in 'special education' and one (7 per cent) was attending a Pupil Referral Unit. None of the children was able to report any significant educational achievement or qualification.

- Five (33 per cent) of the children reported having received formal psychiatric treatment and almost all of the children referred to episodes of 'depression', 'self-harm' and 'suicidal thoughts' in the course of the interviews.
- Almost all the children reported drinking alcohol and/or using illicit drugs. Ten (67 per cent) of the children reported having experienced 'serious problems' as a result of drinking alcohol, and seven (47 per cent) reported 'serious drug use'.

Vulnerability, as discussed on pp. 6–8, is itself a complex term, which is difficult to define. According to recent draft guidance published by the Department of Health, vulnerable children are those 'who have acquired or encountered some difficulty which requires additional help if their life chances are to be optimised or the risk of social exclusion is to be averted' (cited in Newbronner, 2002: 40). Indeed, the children recognise their vulnerabilities, and the vulnerabilities of others in secure accommodation, as shown in their responses to the statement, 'Young people in secure units are sometimes described as vulnerable.' On a five-point scale, ranging from 'strongly agree' to 'strongly disagree', three children (20 per cent) elected 'strongly agree' with the remaining 12 (80 per cent) opting for 'mostly agree'. The children were asked to explain their responses:

Staying out late at night and staying at people's houses. They are at risk with people that they don't even know and no-one else knows that they are there. They don't know what might happen.

(Girl aged 12)

Some definitely are because they haven't had a chance. They have never had a chance. (Girl aged 14)

Some have no-one to talk to about their problems, no-one to help them with their problems. (Girl aged 14)

I think I agree in some ways. I think some kids are unsafe. Some are placed in here because Social Services think we're at risk but we're not, but I suppose some are. Kids who are really messing themselves up and that, cutting their arms and that. (Boy aged 15)

Such responses focus primarily upon the 'situational vulnerability' of children in potentially dangerous circumstances and are consistent with the emphases in the comments made by the Secure Unit staff. However, other children, while recognising the prevalence of such situational vulnerability, also introduce the perceived significance of their looked-after status. They contend that being in care *in itself* compounds the likelihood of being placed in secure accommodation. They effectively question the legitimacy of professional licence and the associated exercise of discretionary power. In other words, the children argue that they are discriminated against on the very basis of their looked-after status, and their relative powerlessness (as children in care) is thus experienced as a form of structural vulnerability:

You can't really look after yourself and you easily get dragged into stuff. I'm only in secure because I've been in the care system since I was four. If I wasn't in the care system I wouldn't be sat here now . . . it's only because I'm in care that they can do this to me. Everyone is vulnerable at some point in their lives but they won't be dragged into secure units. It's because I'm in care. I am vulnerable but I wouldn't be here if I wasn't in care . . . (Girl aged 14)

Vulnerable, I've been called vulnerable, putting myself at risk, self-harming and that . . . it's just words – it doesn't mean nothing. It's labelling us that's what they do, Social Services. They just blag the judges' heads. Who are Social Services to judge us? They just twist everything around, they label things to suit their own purposes.
(Girl aged 14)

. . . They've always told me that I'm vulnerable. They say I can't look after myself because of my age but age is nothing to do with it. Since the age of 11 I've been running off and looking after myself. When you're in care they don't care about you. That's their job but they're just there and you have to look after yourself. I'm not like a normal 15-year-old girl who has had a family and never run off . . . OK I might have made mistakes and got into bad situations but it pisses me right off when they say I'm too young to look after myself . . . Some kids are vulnerable and some aren't . . . You learn

as you go along how to do things, how to look after yourself, how to
survive. When there is no-one else to look after you you've got to
look after yourself so you can't be vulnerable then can you?

(Girl aged 15)

This introduces a further layer of complexity which some of the
Independent Persons and Guardians *ad litem*/Children's Guardians
also identified in their interviews. Typical comments include:

It is surprising how many local authorities are unclear about the
criteria for secure accommodation. They have very different
approaches, different ways of understanding vulnerability – there is
no real consistent definition as to what constitutes vulnerability.
The most obvious example is gender differences: girls are much
more likely to be locked up if they are out on the streets. It is far
too difficult to come up with a concrete definition. They can
become more vulnerable by staying in a secure placement and
becoming over-dependent upon the structure of the unit.

(Independent Person)

It's pretty subjective and there are lots of problems. For example the
concerns are higher at 12 rather than 15 or 16, yet the younger they
go in the more likely they are to go back. There is an increased use
of secure accommodation if there is a serious incident or a death.
It is probably more to do with how Social Services are worried about
looking, if something goes wrong, than worry about the child. That is
cynical but it is probably true as well. (GALRO/Children's Guardian)

To sum up, the typical circumstances and background characteristics
of children in secure accommodation, as described by the staff,
together with the social profiles of the interview sample of children,
present a distressing picture, which accords with 'official' definitions
of vulnerability. Moreover, the children themselves have little
difficulty in recognising their own vulnerabilities, and the
vulnerabilities of others in secure accommodation. Whether or not
such vulnerabilities warrant placements in locked institutions raises
far more complex considerations. Indeed, some of the children
passionately suggest that it is their looked-after status, more so than
their actual behaviours, which determines their placement into secure

accommodation. Equally, some of the Independent Persons and Guardians *ad litem*/Children's Guardians interviewed referred to related issues. These included: inconsistencies in the interpretation and application of formal criteria; subjective and differential definitions of vulnerability between local authorities; gendered and age-related patterns of vulnerability; the potential for secure accommodation to compound rather than alleviate vulnerability; and the relation between organisational imperatives and Secure Order applications. Such issues echo the concerns examined in Chapter 2 (*see* pp. 23–34) and they will be further considered throughout this chapter. The same issues raise formidable questions for policy and practice, and their very complexity defies conclusive answers. What is more certain, however, is that the processes of vulnerability assessment, and the pressured contexts within which assessments are found, tend to impede the practices of partnership and consultation, and invariably serve to exclude children's perspectives. It is this which will now be considered.

ASSESSING VULNERABILITY: THE 'WISHES AND FEELINGS OF THE CHILD', CONSULTATION, PARTNERSHIP AND PLACEMENT

The children were asked if anyone had discussed secure accommodation with them before the application for an Order was made to the court.

Seven (47 per cent) of the children explained that they had been given an indication that an application for a Secure Accommodation Order was being, or might be, made. Moreover, some of these children had clearly been consulted at length and in good time. Their comments included:

I asked to come in here to get off the drugs and get myself together. I had to get away from everything and they helped me.
(Girl aged 15)

They told me loads of times that unless I stopped running away they would put a claim in for secure accommodation. I knew that I would be coming here. (Girl aged 12)

Others had been notified but with little or no meaningful consultation:

They had been going on and they had said that I'd be going to secure but I didn't really know that they were applying for the order.
(Girl aged 14)

They told me just before I had to come but they knew a long time before that. They said this was a positive move but I didn't think it was because I'd been in secure before and it did no good. I thought that they were making the wrong decision but they didn't really listen so I just went along with it. I thought, 'Why have they waited? Why have they just decided to spring it on me like that?', but I suppose they had to in case I did a runner. (Boy aged 15)

However, eight (53 per cent) of the children explained that they were completely unaware of the arrangements that Social Services had made. Clearly some of the Secure Unit admissions had been made in crisis situations, when it would have been exceptionally difficult to consult with the child, for example:

I was upset and angry. They put me in here for 72 hours and then I had to go to court. (Girl aged 14)

It wasn't explained to me at all. I had taken an overdose and I was brought here straight from hospital. I was really worried. I didn't even know what one looked like. I'd never been in one before, never even seen one. (Girl aged 16)

I'd been running off all the time and one of the times I ran off the police got me and put me in a police cell. My social worker said that I was going to secure. I was upset and really, really angry. I was scratching myself like mad and I felt like killing myself.
(Girl aged 13)

In other cases, however, the admissions appeared to be organised to deliberately deceive the child:

My social worker and three escorts came and said, 'We are going to take you somewhere.' I didn't know where I was going until I got here. I was so upset I couldn't even speak. (Girl aged 15)

*I didn't know that I was coming here. They told me that I was going
to an open unit. I had some idea that something weird was going on
but the escorts were saying all the way, 'We are not taking you to a
secure unit you know, we are taking you to an open unit'. They said,
'We're not paid to lie' but they did, they brought me here.*

(Girl aged 14)

*They should have told me that I was coming to this place rather than
just putting me in here. I found out when I got to the place and I saw
the big fence and was taken into the garage. I thought, 'Oh no, what
is this place?' I thought I was coming to a children's home but it had
this massive fence and everything was locked up. (Boy aged 16)*

It would be wrong to underestimate the pressure on social workers
(practitioners and managers), when a manifestly vulnerable child
repeatedly exposes her/himself to serious danger. Indeed, it would be
utterly irresponsible for Social Services not to take decisive action to
safeguard children in such cases. It is not necessarily unreasonable,
therefore, should crisis circumstances require, for social workers to
take action without fully consulting the child. Despite this, the
apparent regularity, nature and extent to which consultation with
children is suspended during the procedures leading to applications
for welfare placements in secure accommodation, raises serious
concerns relating to the provisions of statute, professional ethics,
human rights and the established conventions of best child-care
practice. The liberty of the child is at stake in such circumstances and
every effort should be made to reach resolutions that take the fullest
account of her/his 'wishes and feelings', in order to 'safeguard and
promote' her/his welfare and avoid unnecessary restriction of liberty.
To do otherwise is tantamount to professional abuse.

Of course children do have the benefit of a Guardian *ad litem*/
Children's Guardian in secure accommodation proceedings as
discussed in Chapter 2 (*see* pp. 15–16). The primary duties of the
Guardian *ad litem*/Children's Guardian are to safeguard the interests
of the child; to ensure that the child has an effective voice in court by
representing her/his 'ascertainable wishes and feelings'; to try to
avoid delays in the case being heard and/or determined, and to have
regard to the 'welfare checklist' as provided by Section 1 of the

Children Act 1989. This could comprise a solid foundation upon which the interests and rights of the child might be guaranteed. However, in practice this can all look rather different as some of the interviews with the Guardians *ad litem*/Children's Guardians illustrated:

> You have got to believe what you are told essentially and what is in the reports. The best you can hope for is 72 hours' notice to prepare. You often have to see the child in the court, such is the shortage of notice and this usually means interviewing them in the court cells. What on earth are kids on welfare grounds doing in such cells? I once had to do a case with only ten minutes' warning.
>
> *(GALRO/Children's Guardian)*

> The problem is with the criteria. If this is met then there is little option in terms of the time available for the GALRO/Children's Guardian to suggest alternatives. Some Guardians find it very challenging. There is so little time to make a difference.
>
> *(GALRO/Children's Guardian)*

> I am never very popular with the local authority if I say I am going to oppose the application. I had one case where the social worker said to me, 'If you don't agree to this the child will die.' Where do you go with that? Sometimes it is in the best interests of the child to manage the risk in the community, however. This is all down to how much the social worker is prepared to take the risk . . .
>
> *(GALRO/Children's Guardian)*

Clearly the circumstances in which the Guardians *ad litem*/ Children's Guardians are required to operate are unlikely to provide sufficient opportunity for meaningful consultation with children. The combination of short notice and compressed timescales, minimal background knowledge and information, and highly charged environments, are hardly conducive to seeking the 'wishes and feelings' of the child or reaching a balanced and objective assessment of vulnerability. Indeed, where there is so little engagement and consultation with children, it is not surprising that most of the interviewees felt aggrieved with the process and took a fundamentally different view to that of the professionals.

The children were asked whether or not they agreed with the

Secure Accommodation Order. Only two (13 per cent) agreed; one (seven per cent) was uncertain and the overwhelming majority, 12 (80 per cent), disagreed. The two children who agreed with the Order explained that they recognised that they needed 'time-out', and that they thought that secure accommodation would provide them with an opportunity to break from circumstances that had moved beyond their control. The child who was uncertain commented:

I didn't really agree at the time but I thought that I would just go along with it. They got a three-month Order but now they say they are going to go for another one and I will get my solicitor to challenge that. That's not what they said. That's not what we agreed. (Boy aged 15)

Comments of the 12 children who disagreed included:

They are keeping me in here now for three months and I don't think it is right to be locked up. I have not broken the law – I have just run away and I am now locked up. That's not right. (Girl aged 15)

I disagreed because I was in care voluntarily and they shouldn't force me to be locked up. (Girl aged 14)

I didn't think that it would really help me or anything or make any difference. It was just about being locked up so they didn't have to worry about me. (Girl aged 14)

I didn't agree because I was trying my best to keep myself safe. I thought that I could go to a Children's Home. I shouldn't have been lied to. I should have been told the truth and I might have settled in more. Being lied to is not very nice. My social worker lied to me.
(Boy aged 16)

The child's role within the overall process leading to placement in secure accommodation is apparently marginal. Most of the children who were interviewed reported an antagonistic and adversarial experience as distinct from conciliatory partnership. It is difficult to imagine how such children must feel on arrival at the Secure Unit, how they first view its purpose and function, and how they may reconcile the placement in terms of safeguarding and promoting their care and welfare.

CONCEPTUALISING THE PURPOSE AND FUNCTION OF SECURE ACCOMMODATION

The children were asked what they imagined the Secure Unit would be like when they were told that they were to be admitted. Typical responses included:

> I was scared because I didn't know where I was going and I thought that the girls and staff would be really horrible. I'd heard a few things about secure and being locked up 24/7 and I was scared. I was scared in case everyone was horrible to me. *(Girl aged 12)*

> I thought that the kids would be bullies. I was worried that there would be bullies. I was worried about the staff because I didn't know any of them. They said it wasn't safe living where I was, but at least I'd known them for years. *(Boy aged 14)*

The children were also asked how they felt when they arrived at the unit:

> When I got to this place and got out the car I first saw a fence and then I really realised they'd brought me to a secure unit. I just walked in quietly and they searched me. I was very, very upset and depressed. I was shocked and frightened. I didn't know how long I was staying here and when I was going to get out. I thought I might have to stay here forever. It was dead horrible and frightening.
>
> *(Girl aged 15)*

> I was thinking, 'Is this place going to be a nice place or is it going to be a horrible place?' When I came in, I thought, 'Is this prison?' . . . The first thing I saw was all the locks and really big doors and I thought, 'What have they brought me to here?' There is this fence and it makes you feel really closed in. *(Boy aged 16)*

> I felt terrified, I had really bad butterflies in my stomach. I just wanted to go home where I belong. I just thought, 'Look what I've landed myself in.' I didn't think Social Services would dare put me in here. I didn't cry in front of them but when I got to my room I was crying. *(Girl aged 12)*

I was really angry. I don't know what I felt really, I was really upset though. They had lied to me and told me that I was going to an open unit when they knew all along that they were going to put me here. I just felt like I couldn't trust anybody. (Girl aged 14)

I was crying. I was really upset. I was kicking off and that. I was swearing and all that. I had to take everything off and have a shower. All my jewellery was taken off me. No-one was with me who I know. I thought, 'Most probably, I'll be in here forever.'
(Girl aged 13)

The sense of profound trepidation and fearful anticipation characterises the responses of the children. Moreover, their anxieties appear to be confirmed on arrival at the Secure Units where high perimeter fences, locked doors and associated security systems and procedures symbolise all of their worse fears. There is little evidence to suggest that such vulnerable children initially see secure accommodation as a place of safety within which they will be looked after and protected. The contrast between the experiences of children on one hand, and professional views of secure accommodation on the other, is quite striking. The overwhelming majority of the children interviewed initially saw secure accommodation as punitive and fear-inducing, whereas the staff almost all emphasised child-centred welfare priorities provided within a context of security:

The main purpose is to keep children safe . . . It is about taking some of the control away from them, because we work with children who have been given so much freedom and opportunity, and so little control, that they have pressed the self-destruct button.
(Secure Unit Residential Social Worker)

We have to start with the basics of keeping them alive. Sometimes the child needs to be in a situation that they can't run from in order to begin to address their problems. It can be as basic as primary health care, and from there you can move on to addressing the core problems of abuse, child prostitution, etc. It can be about providing relief, about providing a safe haven. For some children this will be the first time that they are being heard. It can be about helping

children to find their talents. The first time that we see them for what they are rather than the problems associated with them.
                                                    (Secure Unit Manager)

Firstly to ensure the child's safety. All our kids are first and foremost children. We can offer a child-centred approach that keeps children safe and does intensive work around their difficulties. I am not suggesting that we can resolve such difficulties but we give them an opportunity to make decisions. We also give them an opportunity to be a child because many of these kids have been denied a childhood.   (Secure Unit Manager)

I hate the negative connotations about secure accommodation as a last resort. We see it as a continuum of care: an opportunity to provide a new start for a child.   (Secure Unit Manager)

The whole ethos is about preparation for re-entering the community, and enhance their self-esteem and self-worth.
                                              (Secure Unit Deputy Manager)

Such contrasting views of secure accommodation are inevitably over-simplified. The children's perspectives above relate to their *initial* views of secure accommodation. Bearing in mind that, by definition, such children are placed in Secure Units in crisis conditions, and with the barest of consultation, their antipathy is to be expected. There is also evidence to suggest that, once settled, some children begin to see some benefit in their placement:

It will give me time to think about what I'm going to do when I get out. I need to prove that I can be trusted. It keeps me safe as well, in a way. The more I'm here the more I have a chance to build a future for myself. (Girl aged 14)

They are teaching me how to behave normal rather than do stupid things. They are giving me education and that. I wasn't going to school on the outside so I suppose it's better now. (Girl aged 14)

It has helped me because I have not run away from my problems and the staff here can spend more time with you to help you with your problems. (Girl aged 16)

It's got me off the drugs and I've cleaned myself up a bit, and I feel much healthier, and I'm going to start college when I get out.

(Girl aged 15)

It would be wrong to caricature *all* children as being implacably opposed to secure accommodation, just as it would be misleading to suggest that *all* staff share an unquestioning faith in their practice. Nevertheless, there is a mismatch of views at the root of which lie the complex questions of legitimacy and efficacy. To what extent is it legitimate to lock up children in order to 'help' them? To what extent is secure accommodation appropriate for addressing children's vulnerabilities? The efficacy of secure accommodation will be considered towards the end of this chapter (*see* pp. 122–124), but the question of legitimacy will be considered first.

ADDRESSING VULNERABILITY THROUGH 'INCARCERATIVE CHILD-CARE'

During the process of interviews, the secure accommodation staff were invited to respond to the question: 'To what extent is it legitimate to lock up children for welfare purposes?' To collate their responses a scale was used offering four options: 'entirely legitimate', 'partially legitimate', 'not legitimate' and 'uncertain'. Staff responded by choosing one of the first two options, with 11 (55 per cent) choosing the 'entirely legitimate' option and the remaining nine (45 per cent) opting for 'partially legitimate'.

Of the staff who felt that civil/welfare placements in Secure Units are 'entirely legitimate' typical comments included:

Young people are not secured on welfare grounds for singing out of tune in the choir. We do not secure children at the drop of a hat. The kids here are all at serious risk and if locking them up means that we can keep them safe then so be it. (Secure Unit Shift Manager)

I suppose that this is best explained by referring to specific examples. Take the young girl here at the moment, just 13 years old and heavily into child prostitution in London. We have to get kids like that safe and settled. How far can it be left to go before her life is

*lost either to adult control and abuse or literally lost. We have to help
her to be a child again. Another example is serious self-harm issues.
It seems ludicrous to lock such kids up but it can be the only way to
keep them alive and to me that makes it legitimate. Many of these
kids need us to take control. That sounds very punitive but it can be
the only bloody way of keeping them alive. (Secure Unit Manager)*

*I work in a Secure Unit so I have to think that it is legitimate.
For a lot of children it is here or we are going to end up reading
about them in the paper some day because they will end up dead.
Here it gives them a chance to reflect upon their situation and the
consequences of their behaviour.*

(Secure Unit Residential Social Worker)

*I understand the human rights issues but I am just a simple person
working in a Secure Unit with kids in crisis. I've been to several
children's funerals and I don't like it. (Secure Unit Shift Manager)*

Indeed, *all* the staff who opted for the 'entirely legitimate' option
stressed the crisis conditions that beset children before admission,
together with their sense of professional responsibility to protect
them. Many staff emphasised life-death scenarios and felt that secure
accommodation was the *only* means to provide adequate safeguards
for such children. However, the staff who chose the 'partially
legitimate' option (while recognising the points made by their
colleagues and sharing some of their protective pragmatism) also
raised a number of pressing concerns including:

*It is very questionable at times whether or not all of the alternatives
have been explored. (Secure Unit Residential Social Worker)*

*I think that secure orders are abused and generally welfare kids are
here for far too long. Generally efforts are not made to get them
out quickly enough. Part of the problem is that more creative ways
of dealing with the kids and their difficulties might be more
appropriate. We have had kids locked up here in order to give the
Social Worker time to find a bed for them. That is absolutely
obscene. We had a child here, just ten years old, for three-and-a-half
months because they couldn't find an open placement.*

(Secure Unit Residential Social Worker)

Whilst it is deemed to be in the best interests of the child other issues are also at stake including back-covering. There are some young people who will always run and will always be exposed to serious risks. However, there are times when Social Services choose to cover their backs and at such times the kids end up here.

(Secure Unit Team Leader)

I worry about it all the time . . . You are touching on issues of human rights. They haven't done anything illegal but a magistrate deems that they need locking up for their own safety. For the kid it is their life and they think that they should be able to do what they want with it . . . A question that I ask myself is that as an adult if I did the same behaviour would I be locked up for my own good? In most cases I wouldn't. It's a question of rights and who has the right to decide what is best. It is really difficult.

(Secure Unit Residential Social Worker)

If you don't lock some of them up they would definitely be dead. Locking them up is the only way to keep them safe. A lot of the kids argue that, 'You can't lock me up for ever and I am going to be the same when I get out so why not let me out now?' If I am honest they have a point you know.

(Secure Unit Residential Social Worker).

Four issues are particularly noteworthy in the concerns raised by these staff. First is the question of alternative resources, both for the purposes of avoiding recourse to secure accommodation, and to facilitate the earliest discharge of children who are placed in Secure Units. Second is the balance between agency/professional interests and the interests of the child. Third is the question of power and rights, particularly in relation to determining whether or not the child should have their liberty withdrawn. Fourth is the efficacy consideration and the extent to which secure accommodation makes any medium-term impact to the benefit of the child. The question of children's rights was considered earlier (at least in part) and will be returned to shortly in relation to Secure Accommodation Reviews. The question of efficacy is raised towards the end of this chapter, but alternative resources and agency priorities are now considered.

Many of the children interviewed felt that their difficulties could have been addressed more effectively without restricting their liberty:

> There should be more support from Social Workers and Social Services generally. I needed counselling and somebody to help me to come to terms with everything that had happened to me. My Social Worker tried her best but she was always too busy . . . They should have Social Workers who can give kids proper attention rather than always having to go and do loads of other things. Look now, I am locked up in here and it's costing them loads and loads of money. I'm not happy and I bet they're not happy with what it's costing them. If I had had proper help it may not have got to this. . .
>
> (Girl aged 16)

> I don't know. I haven't figured it out yet but there must be better ways in this world without sticking us in Secure Units. You need people who kids can trust, I know that much. (Girl aged 14)

> I think that they should really try every other form of placement before you come in here. Once you've been in secure it's easy for them to put you back in so they stop thinking of anything else.
>
> (Girl aged 14)

A common feature of what the children were saying was the need for sustained and perhaps even quite intensive support that would be *responsive* to their *needs* as distinct from *reactive* to their *behaviour*. However, the children also perceived the pressure and competing demands upon case-workers who they felt were unable to provide the level of support they needed. Similarly, the Independent Persons and the Guardians *ad litem*/Children's Guardians expressed frustrations with the limited alternatives, tight resources and the pressures that mainstream Children's Services are under:

> We really need to think of children in the way in which we would want to see our own children treated. To view these kids as human beings with major problems, as children who need to be nurtured. However, there do not appear to be any alternatives available. Too often they seem to be scrubbing around with nowhere to place them. It is an increasingly fragmented system, which increasingly gives up on kids. Residential services are under-funded, with poor

staff morale and high staff turnover. That is just no good for these kids. (Independent Person)

It is a real problem – the lack of resources. A major problem relates to Child and Adolescent Mental Health Services. There is some very poor practice in residential care and what happens is that the kids get sent out to private placements out-of-city. Some of them are good but many are very poor. I think that properly resourced foster placements, and I mean properly resourced, is a real possibility. We need to pay people though to do the job and provide back-up support services and at the moment neither of those things appear to be available. (GALRO/Children's Guardian)

From the accounts provided by children, Secure Unit staff, Independent Persons and Guardians *ad litem*/Children's Guardians, the legitimacy of secure accommodation (in its welfare application) begins to look quite shaky. Of course the official guidance and regulations explicitly refer to the need to protect children from 'unnecessary and inappropriate placement in secure accommodation' (Department of Health, 1993: para 8.9), and it also provides that 'all else must first have been comprehensively considered and rejected [and] never because no other placement was available at the relevant time' (*ibid*: para 8.5). However, a key message to emerge from the interviews is that 'all else' often doesn't amount to very much, and that admissions to secure accommodation are regularly premised upon the non-availability of 'other placements'. This is not to deny the various crises that beset children, nor the best efforts of the professionals involved, but it does resonate with the concerns that were raised in Chapter 2 (*see* pp. 23–28), particularly relating to system failure on the one hand, and the organisational interests of Social Services Departments on the other. Indeed, in many cases, it would seem that secure accommodation is little more than a stop-gap, a temporary bolt-hole to stave off an organisational problem – a point made both implicitly and explicitly in many interviews not least by the Guardians *ad litem*/Children's Guardians:

There is real pressure on resources so the social worker can't get what the kid needs, nor give what they need. It's all about money and budgetary pressure. However, as soon as something goes wrong or begins to look really hairy then the assistant director can find the money, no problem. As soon as things begin to look dodgy for Social Services the emphasis soon shifts to welfare and they are all calling for Secure. It's warehousing though, that's what it is. It's not horticulture, it's not really for the purposes of meeting the child's real needs. (GALRO/Children's Guardian)

It's all too often professional back-covering – that's what it is.

(GALRO/Children's Guardian)

Therefore, despite all the complexities, the legitimacy of civil/welfare placements in secure accommodation – in many if not all cases – is suspect and open to question. Children who are looked after face the prospect of loss of liberty because the system is unable to meet their needs. Ultimately, such children are vulnerable not only to the perils of the street, but also to the failings of the child-care system and the excesses and misplaced application of professional power. Here the limited safeguards provided by Secure Accommodation Reviews are of crucial importance.

SECURE ACCOMMODATION REVIEWS: SAFEGUARDING CHILDREN'S RIGHTS?

In Chapter 2 (*see* pp. 16–17) it was noted that Regulation 15 of the relevant Statutory Instrument provides that every child placed in a Secure Unit should have her/his case reviewed 'within one month of the inception of the placement and then at intervals not exceeding three months where the child continues to be kept in such accommodation' (Department of Health, 1991). The review is charged with two primary responsibilities: first, to consider whether or not the legal criteria for keeping the child in secure accommodation continue to apply and, second, to assess whether or not such a placement continues to be necessary. For the purposes of conducting each review the local authority is required to appoint at least three people, one of whom should not be employed by the local authority looking after the child or by the local authority managing the secure unit in which the child is held (the 'Independent Person'). Each of the 20 secure accommodation staff interviewed expressed the importance of the Independent Person and typical comments included:

We deal with the day-to-day behaviour and that can cloud the bigger picture. Somebody outside of here who is not the social worker or keyworker is good – some real independence to safeguard the child's interests. (Secure Unit Residential Social Worker)

A lot of time they [the children] are careful what they say to us. A lot of independents are on their side whereas we work for the system that has locked them up.

(Secure Unit Residential Social Worker)

Kids here are vulnerable, not just in themselves but because they are locked up and they need access to external independent people especially at their reviews. (Secure Unit Residential Social Worker)

The presence of an Independent Person is clearly important but it is the degree to which the child feels able to actively participate which is arguably crucial. During the interviews the children were asked, 'How well do the reviews provide you with an opportunity to have your say?' To collate their responses a scale was used offering four options: 'very well', 'quite well', 'not very well' and 'not well at all'. None of the children responded by choosing the 'very well' or 'not well at all' options, ten (67 per cent) chose 'quite well' and five (33 per cent) opted for 'not very well'.

Of the children who chose the 'quite well' option typical comments included:

They give you an opportunity to say what you want to say.

(Girl aged 14)

I speak for myself. Some kids can't and that's why the authority walks all over them. If you don't know what you want and what they're doing is wrong, then they can walk all over you. There was a lass here for fifteen months for welfare. If she'd pushed and pushed they would have had to let her out. It was nearly a three-year sentence, because you only do half for good behaviour, don't you?

(Girl aged 14)

*I can say my bit. There are loads of adults talking about me but
I listen to what they say then I say my bit. (Girl aged 13)*

*I do get a say and they do treat me quite well. They write it all down
what I say and it goes to court as well. But I'm still in here though,
they don't agree with me. They agree with some things sometimes
I suppose, but mostly they don't. (Boy aged 16)*

Even though these children feel that there are opportunities to 'have
their say', they are less convinced that their perspectives are 'heard'
and taken seriously. This view was also shared by the children who
chose the 'not very well' option, who also felt uncomfortable with the
nature of the reviews themselves:

*I don't really say anything because I know that even if I did it
wouldn't be taken into consideration anyway. Social Services don't
listen to your point of view, they do what they want to do. Whether
you challenge it or not they still do what they want to do. Every time
a kid goes in care they are worse off than when they weren't in care.*
(Girl aged 14)

*I find it quite helpful to have an Independent Person there
sometimes because I don't find it that easy to put my view across
at reviews. There's a lot of adults and professionals and just me.
Sometimes it's OK but others it's quite difficult. (Girl aged 16)*

*I had someone to represent me but I don't really know who they are.
It's hard to talk for yourself, you get embarrassed. It's hard when
they speak something personal and confidential out in front of
everyone. It's very embarrassing. (Girl aged 14)*

From a children's rights perspective, even with the presence of an
Independent Person, the review system appears to offer limited
opportunities for children's participation. Furthermore, the extent
to which the rights of children are safeguarded by the reviewing
process is further compromised by the complexities of assessing
whether or not the legal criteria continue to be met, and by
the associated concerns and organisational imperatives discussed
earlier:

It is very easy for a court to consider that a time in secure is good for a child for direct work and assessment to be done but we can't demonstrate really that the criteria continue to be met or not because they are in here. Where is the evidence of how they will be in the community? (Secure Unit Residential Social Worker)

I would hope that we can assess the criteria but there are girls who play the game whilst they're here, but fully intend to get back on the street, so how does the panel jump? Does it go against the fact that they are well behaved and say all the right things when they're here, the written evidence . . . it's more of a general feeling than a precise science. It's all part of calculating the risk. The criteria can be fudged to suit the circumstances. (Secure Unit Manager)

The problem I always have with this is that if a kid is sailing along the decision is made that they don't meet the criteria then they are released, then we have them back in a couple of months. I know you can't lock children up forever but this is very frustrating. On the other hand, we sometimes keep kids when they could manage on the outside. (Secure Unit Shift Leader)

Initially of course the criteria apply. However, it often brings relief for the social worker and they are kept here longer than they have to be. Often there are no alternative placements and a child is kept here even though they don't meet the criteria . . . It can be seen as a bit of a dumping ground. (Secure Unit Assistant Manager)

If you have easy kids there can be some temptation to keep hold of them but what kind of abuse is that? The alternative scenario is Social Services' Departments covering their backs or having insufficient alternatives, so they leave kids which is also an abuse. That's the biggest one, exit plans not being put into place. It is not lawful to keep a child contained because you don't have a placement but it happens. It happens quite a lot actually.
(Secure Unit Manager)

The Secure Unit staff raise a series of important issues about reviews. Many of the staff refer to the complexity of assessing the ongoing applicability of the legal criteria once the child is *in situ*. Some staff recall scenarios in which children who 'play the game' are discharged prematurely. More often, staff describe the tendency for reviews to either 'play safe', or to reach decisions which suit the exigencies of the placing authority and/or the Secure Unit itself, which prolong placements and continue to unduly restrict the liberty of children. The Independent Person clearly fulfils an important and more objective function but, as noted in Chapter 2 (*see* p. 17), despite the independent element of the formal reviewing process, there is no obligation on the placing local authority, and/or the Secure Unit itself, to follow the recommendations of the reviewing panel. The implications can be very significant for children, and as one Independent Person explained in interview, 'I have known situations where local authorities have overturned the unanimous decision of the Review Panel'. Indeed, the Independent Persons are particularly conscious of the limitations of their roles, power and influence:

We often attend these panels with little information and little knowledge of the specific circumstances and the individual child. Without knowledge of the young person it is almost impossible to determine whether the criteria are met. We make efforts to see young people the day before the Review but there are practical problems with this, not least of which is the cost, because we are paid on a fee basis. Time with the young person is obviously crucial but it often boils down to money. (Independent Person)

There is a strong element of tokenism. It is a requirement that an Independent Person is involved but it is going through the motions really. They already know what the decision is going to be. I sometimes think, 'Would it have been any different if I wasn't there?' (Independent Person)

There is a real poverty of alternative provision and it often comes down to that. (Independent Person)

To summarise, secure accommodation staff have no difficulty in recognising the importance of the formal reviewing process and the role of the Independent Person. However, the extent to which such mechanisms safeguard the rights of children, and provide opportunities for their meaningful participation, is questionable.

Some children clearly feel able to contribute actively to the Review Panels, while others' sense of discomfort, intimidation, and/or embarrassment renders them marginal to the proceedings. Almost all the children, however, whether they actively contribute or not, feel that their perspectives are ignored.

Many staff emphasise the complexities and difficulties in assessing the applicability of legal criteria from *within* secure accommodation which is, by definition, an 'unnatural' environment. Furthermore, in practice the reviews apparently court multiple agendas, which extend beyond the question of legal criteria, but which have an equally significant impact upon the child's liberty. This returns to the issues of different organisational interests, power brokering and the inevitable question of resources. In short, the ostensible safeguards provided by secure accommodation reviews have limited practical value, and the rights of the child are overshadowed by machinations and processes over which they have minuscule influence.

CARE OR PUNISHMENT?

As seen earlier, the circumstances in which many children are admitted to secure accommodation, the paradox of incarcerative care, and the relative powerlessness of children within Secure Units, raises formidable and complex issues. Such issues cut to the very essence of secure accommodation and probe its primary purpose. The 'care versus control', and 'welfare versus punishment' debates, are well rehearsed in this respect. However, as discussed in Chapters 2 and 4, such debates have most recently been re-energised by the reform and reconfigured nature of the juvenile secure estate, and the consequent impact of change upon the welfare constituency. Many of the children interviewed had very clear views on this:

Not all of us are in here for our own safety. It's not right that we are mixed – we should be kept separate. DTOs [Detention and Training Orders] and welfare are here for very different reasons and yet we are just all put together. (Girl aged 16)

There should be a unit for those who harm themselves and are on Section 25, and another unit for those on sentence. All the kids in each unit should be there for the same things and it would make it better. Certain staff could work with certain people and

*help them more instead of having to try and work with
everyone.* (Girl aged 14)

Moreover, the children clearly feel that living in closed conditions,
alongside those who have been placed under the provisions of
criminal justice legislation, serves to criminalise them; expose them
to potential danger; subject them to inappropriate regimes; and
impose manifest injustices upon them:

> *I do not think that Section 25 and kids with criminal records should
> be mixed together. I think that I am going to be classed as a criminal.
> If I was 21 I wouldn't be sent to prison on Section 25 to be with
> adults who are criminal. I think that there should be separate units
> for Section 25 and criminals, because criminals are here to serve
> their sentence, and I am here because I was at risk and I shouldn't
> have to mix with people who are here for crime.* (Girl aged 14)

> *Kids who do crime and get four months, they do two months in and
> two months out, and kids on welfare get three months and have to
> do three months straight. I don't think that's fair. Kids on welfare put
> themselves at risk, but kids on crime put others at risk and then only
> do two months. It's not right. I get more time just for putting myself
> at risk.* (Girl aged 14)

The Secure Unit staff express similar concerns and further explain
the implications of placing especially vulnerable children in units
that are increasingly charged with correctional objectives:

> *Generally they think that they are here to be punished. How can you
> explain to a girl who has been abused for years and comes in here
> for self-harming and overdosing that she is not being punished when
> the abuser is walking about freely on the outside? . . . More to the
> point, how do you explain to her that it is not punishment when
> she comes in here and is mixing with children serving sentences?
> We used to be, more or less, Section 25 and all of the girls would be
> very similar, in terms of their backgrounds and circumstances. We
> would have the occasional Section 53, but it was pretty occasional.
> But now it's about half and half, and they are meeting and living with
> girls who have come in for totally different reasons. This also means
> different regimes, which makes it more difficult. The YJB kids have*

to be out of their rooms for a certain number of hours, which means at weekends the doors need to be opened at 8 am whereas the welfare girls want a lie in. It makes managing this very difficult because they are not all doing the same thing. Plus, if the welfare girls get mobility this can wrangle with the DTOs who don't. Sometimes the girls themselves complain that they are mixed with what they call 'criminals'. (Secure Unit Team Leader)

They have to do work which is designed for kids who are here for other reasons and it is not always appropriate. Doing work on offending can raise some very powerful emotional responses for kids who are actually victims, sometimes of nasty offences.
(Secure Unit Residential Social Worker)

Kids and other professionals have asked the question as to why welfare kids should have to do justice programmes . . . The justice system is driving Secure Accommodation. It is a major problem for daily routines now for welfare kids. Welfare kids are now being pulled along by a justice system. (Secure Unit Shift Manager)

A lot of the welfare kids are now using prison-speak such as 'lock down' and 'pads'. We try to discourage that because this is a secure children's home. However, the Youth Justice Board has changed the unit and we now have to try and distinguish in our response to welfare children. (Secure Unit Shift Manager)

Indeed, the reconfigured juvenile secure estate is apparently not only serving to 'squeeze' welfare on the macro level as discussed in Chapter 4 (*see* pp. 86–92), but is also having a major impact at the micro-unit level where regimes and operational practices are increasingly assuming penal identities. Some of the Guardians *ad litem*/Children's Guardians made interesting observations on this:

Some of the kids who enter through Section 25 do not have a criminal history, and they are mixing with offenders in units which are staffed by people who . . . look like bouncers. It's all very macho. It's just like being in prison. It is a children's prison and magistrates don't seem to understand this.
(GALRO/Children's Guardian)

> *The welfare children are now very much in a minority within most of the units. This has lots of implications. For one, it means that within the units it is difficult to meet the needs of welfare children when Youth Justice Board contracts require the staff to spend so much time with children on offending programmes. Another problem is actually finding a welfare bed, which often means that children are placed many miles from their home communities. This is producing a diaspora of welfare cases being spread across what is increasingly becoming a youth justice service. (GALRO/Children's Guardian)*

This all raises some extraordinarily difficult issues. On the one hand, current practice is tantamount to the criminalisation of the most vulnerable children and the creation of utterly inappropriate environments for them (O'Neill, 2001). On the other hand, as will be discussed in Chapter 7, although the welfare and justice constituencies of children enter secure accommodation along quite different legal pathways, their background circumstances and consequent needs are not desperately dissimilar (Goldson, 2000a). This latter point was made by some of the Secure Unit staff:

> *The other way of looking at this is that the justice kids have welfare needs, and we have to be careful not to lose welfare issues for justice kids. (Secure Unit Shift Manager)*

> *When you read the files there is not as much difference in their backgrounds at all. (Secure Unit Team Leader)*

However, despite the similarities between the children, it remains unequivocally inappropriate to expect children whose liberty has been restricted under civil/welfare statute to comply with regimes designed for a fundamentally different purpose. Quite apart from the professional and ethical concerns, there is also the question of efficacy, which will now be considered.

SAFER FUTURES?

The Secure Unit staff were asked whether they felt that children benefit from secure accommodation, and some staff were clearly optimistic:

It keeps them safe. It keeps them alive. It gives them an opportunity for reflection. It gives them an opportunity to be a child again. Some kids, for example, think that they are so tough but we hired a bouncy castle for two days and you should have seen them bouncing and enjoying themselves and being proper kids really.

(Secure Unit Residential Social Worker)

Obviously some don't but more often or not they do. Every single one of the kids arrives looking terrible. We have had kids arriving at 15 who weigh five-and-a-half stone. You can also see their confidence develop. I think that it has some enduring impact too. I think that we have some positive impact on all the kids.

(Secure Unit Residential Social Worker)

Such optimism was shared by some of the children:

I've learned how to deal and cope with my problems. It's helped me trust adults more, both males and females. (Girl aged 16)

If I hadn't come in here I could be dead now. I have a future ahead of me now. I had no future when I got in here. I have to think ahead now but before I just worked from day-to-day. That's the big difference – I've got a future now. (Girl aged 15)

The emphasis here, of course, is placed upon the *immediate* benefits of secure accommodation. In this sense the Secure Unit provides a sojourn, a 'breathing space', as one Independent Person put it, facilitating temporary relief from the dangers of the street: an opportunity to attend to primary health needs; a pit-stop within which to restore a sense of 'childhood'; a chance to re-build emotional well-being and self-worth, however fragile it might prove to be. However, in terms of the medium- to longer-term benefits of secure accommodation, some of the staff and the children were less certain:

There is a real problem with moving on. They can be moved straight back into the situation from where they've come and everything that has been achieved is immediately lost. For some local authorities they are moved straight back to the same situation and you have to ask, 'What on earth is this all about?' (Secure Unit Manager)

The pull of external influence and the peer group is far more important than what they might learn in here and very rarely is there any significant adult in their lives and, even rarer, the same kind of consistent support. Let's face it – loads of them leave with no school to go to. (Secure Unit Shift Manager)

Whilst they are here they are safe and that is the only real benefit. The Social Services Departments get more out of it than the children. It's back-covering. However, the short-term gains are exactly that, short-term, before they start off on the cycle again. The real question you should be asking is, 'Should they be here in the first place?' We are not really addressing their problem – just taking them away from it for a while.

(Secure Unit Residential Social Worker)

The children added:

If you're vulnerable and you come in here it isn't going to make you unvulnerable is it? Just because I'm in here isn't going to change being vulnerable when I get out. I have to learn that on the outside, not in here. I have to have help when I get out but it wasn't there when I came in and it probably won't be when I get out.

(Girl aged 14)

I'm not sure that it will help me. I'm not sure about it, but there's a feeling that it has a bit . . . I've seen girls come back here again so what's the point of staying here if it's just going to be the same again? What has happened in the past can never change, ever ever again . . . It will be the same when I get out . . . that is the problem.

(Girl aged 15)

I have been in here too long. I have not been in the world enough. I don't know what it will be like. I need to be in the world more.

(Boy aged 16)

Indeed, as noted in Chapter 2 (*see* p. 32), very little is known about the medium- to long-term outcomes for children who have been placed in secure accommodation under the provisions of civil/welfare statute. It seems quite extraordinary that under civil proceedings children continue to be placed in institutions that deprive them of their liberty upon such a tentative evidential base. This will be considered again in Chapter 7.

CHAPTER 6

Children, vulnerability and prison

PRISON FROM THE INSIDE

The practice of remanding children in prisons is well established, as discussed in Chapter 3. As has also been observed, there are significant grounds for concern about such practice, and the same concerns provide good reason to bring it to an end. The history of youth justice has been characterised by the determined efforts of penal reform agencies, child welfare organisations and government itself, to substantially reform – if not completely abolish – prison remands for children. There have been periods of tangible progress, perhaps none greater than the inclusion of the provisions in the Criminal Justice Act 1991, which aimed to abolish prison remands for 15- to 16-year-old boys. However, despite the concerns – and the efforts to allay them – and irrespective of statutory provisions and associated international conventions, standards, treaties and rules (*see* Chapter 3), the practice of remanding children in prisons has not only endured, it has also intensified. Indeed, Donovan (2002: 16) recently offered a reminder that 'the number of 15- and 16-year-olds being remanded into prison custody during the past nine years has tripled'. Furthermore, despite the best efforts of those involved, the latest wide-ranging reforms of the juvenile secure estate have made limited impact on improving practice with vulnerable children on penal remands (*see* Chapter 4).

Today, child crime is rarely out of the news, and it might be concluded that the increased use of penal remands for children simply reflects both an increased volume of child crime and an increased gravity. However, there is little evidence to support such assumptions (Goldson, 2002). Moreover, although there can be no doubt that some children commit serious offences and pose significant risks to themselves and/or others (*see* pp. 155 and 158), prison remands are not necessarily reserved for such children. Indeed, the 'seriousness' criteria has recently been significantly diluted by the implementation of Section 130 of the Criminal Justice and Police Act 2001 (*see* pp. 43–44). This was further confirmed during interviews and consultations with managers and practitioners from The Children's Society National Remand Review Initiative (NRRI). The 15 NRRI staff who were interviewed were asked if their experience suggested that prison remands are being reserved for the most serious and/or dangerous child offenders. Only one interviewee (7 per cent) felt this to be the case with the remaining 14 (93 per cent) reporting otherwise. Typical comments included:

I have just interviewed a boy on a £9.99 shop theft. They are persistent and a nuisance but no real threat to the public at all. It is the persistence of their offending which now makes the remand legal but it is quite unnecessary. (NRRI Practitioner)

A lot of kids who we get in have committed a fair quantity of crime but they are not desperately serious, so much so that you wonder how they have met the criteria for custody, but they have been put down as persistent young offenders. As an example, and I admit that it's an extreme example, but I had a kid with learning disabilities who had been remanded for theft of toffees from a toffee jar, and criminal damage to the lid of the jar. (NRRI Practitioner)

This chapter explores some of the core concerns that have been raised around prison remands for children. By setting out the qualitative research findings drawn from the interviews, the comments made by prison personnel, NRRI staff and the children themselves communicate the vulnerabilities of child remand prisoners, their experiences of the remand process, and the realities of life inside Young Offender Institutions.

Twenty-five children (boys aged 15–16 years) held on remand wings in four Young Offender Institutions in England were interviewed. Similarly, interviews were held with 20 Prison Service staff drawn from the same Young Offender Institutions (including governor grade prison officers, principal officers, senior officers and basic-grade officers, together with health and education staff and prison chaplains). Finally, 15 members of staff (operational managers and practitioners) were interviewed from the NRRI (in the North West of England, London, the West Midlands, and Yorkshire and Humberside).

VULNERABLE CHILDREN

The social circumstances of the children who steadily fill our prisons are invariably scarred by multiple and inter-locking forms of disadvantage and misery, the detail of which is discussed in Chapters 3 and 7. Such children are both innately vulnerable and structurally vulnerable, and black children are especially susceptible, challenged by racism and its insidious expressions of social and criminal injustice. A range of assessment processes have recently been implemented in order to identify, 'screen out' and divert the most vulnerable children from the prison system but, as concluded in Chapter 4, such processes are pitted with problems. The juvenile secure estate is simply unable to provide alternative placements for such children, and the vulnerability 'safety net' has gaping holes.

Both NRRI staff and prison personnel recognise the vulnerabilities of child remand prisoners. In interviews, each group of staff was invited to respond to the statement: 'It has been suggested that juvenile remand prisoners are the most vulnerable group of prisoners in the prison system.' On a five-point scale ('agree', 'partially agree', 'partially disagree', 'disagree', 'don't know'), the NRRI and prison staff responded quite similarly. Of the 15 NRRI staff interviewed, eight (53 per cent) agreed with the statement, with the remaining seven (47 per cent) partially agreeing. Of the 20 prison staff interviewed, seven (35 per cent) agreed, 12 (60 per cent) partially agreed and only one (5 per cent) disagreed.

For those who agreed with the interview statement typical explanatory comments included:

I totally agree with it. First off, it's very often the first time they've been in a place like this. For a lot of them it's the first time they've been away from home. Adolescence is a confusing time anyway for, shall we say, normal kids but the vast majority of these kids have had horrendous experiences. (Senior Prison Officer)

I strongly agree, especially for first-timers, and let's not forget that some may be innocent. They have such limited coping mechanisms, poor communication, fear and often deteriorating mental health. Add to this their age, stage of development, prison regime, shock, size of the place, numbers, meeting new adults within concrete boundaries, how can anyone say anything other than they are vulnerable?
(NRRI Operational Manager)

I think that when the door closes and there is no-one else around, the bravado goes and they realise that they are just children. The thought of me being locked up alone when I was 15, it would have scared the hell out of me. That's when they become frightened. The thing with remand, as well, is not knowing how long you are going to get so they are left just to sit and think about that. The remand side is always more unsettled and that applies even more to juveniles. (Prison Officer)

The comments from the staff who were most certain about the vulnerabilities of child remand prisoners echo many of the themes that were discussed in Chapters 3 and 4: the damaged backgrounds; the traumatic experiences; the impact of separation from all that is familiar; the ambiguous legal status (even the possibility of innocence); the deteriorating mental health; the sham veneer of machismo; the uncertainty; and the stark solitude of the cell with only child-like anxiety for company.

For those who partially agreed with the interview statement, explanations included:

*Juvenile remands are vulnerable but there are others who are very vulnerable too. In my experience **all** black prisoners are very vulnerable because of the racist treatment that they receive.*
(NRRI Practitioner)

The remanded kids are extremely vulnerable but in some senses they are better off than the sentenced kids who are often just as vulnerable, but they don't get the same legal visits, the same number of family visits and they have no voluntary organisations such as ourselves to see them. They simply get swallowed up inside the prison. (NRRI Practitioner)

Yes, the juveniles are vulnerable but you have to remember that we have just as many vulnerable prisoners in the young offender group, right up to the age of 21. They might be a little older but the conditions for them are much worse than for the juveniles. (Senior Prison Officer)

It depends what they have on the outside, and that applies to all prisoners. For those who have nothing – and there's a lot of them – the situation is very bleak. (Prison Officer)

There is no denying the vulnerability of child remand prisoners in the comments above, but these staff are more cautious about hierarchies of vulnerability. They appear to recognise the vulnerabilities of juvenile remands just as readily as their ostensibly more certain colleagues, but they also draw attention to different 'coping' mechanisms and the vulnerabilities of other groups of prisoners including black inmates, sentenced juveniles and the young offender group (17–21 years). In some important respects, juvenile remand prisoners – despite their obvious vulnerabilities – are 'better off' than these other groups of prisoners, according to the staff quoted above. However, *all* the interviewees recognised the vulnerabilities of child remand prisoners, whether or not they believed them to be more or less acute than those of other groups of prisoners. Even the single prison officer who disagreed with the interview statement qualified his 'disagreement' in this way, by explaining that the 'first time in custody induces fear in anyone, young or old, male or female'.

Child remand prisoners go through a multi-staged process of 'assessment' during their passage from court to custody (*see* pp. 74–83). During this process each child is repeatedly interviewed by different and unfamiliar adults, who will each raise (however superficially) difficult personal issues with them. With this in mind, the interviews with children for this research explicitly aimed to avoid detailed probing into their personal histories and/or offending profiles. The children were invited to provide some *standard* background information, however, and the results provide an insight into their vulnerabilities:

- The interview sample comprised seven (28 per cent) boys aged 15, and 18 (72 per cent) boys aged 16.

- Just before their penal remands only three (12 per cent) of the boys were living with both parents; seven (28 per cent) were living with their mothers; one (4 per cent) was living with his father; and two (8 per cent) were living with older brothers. The remaining 12 boys (48 per cent) were living apart from any member of their family. One (4 per cent) boy had his own bedsit; two (8 per cent) were lodging with friends; three (12 per cent) were being looked after by local authorities; two (8 per cent) were living in hostel accommodation for homeless young people; and four (12 per cent) were 'on the street', with no fixed abode.

- Most boys reported having histories of formal contact with Social Services for welfare reasons, and of these, ten (40 per cent) were 'open cases' with child-care services when remanded.

- Only four (16 per cent) of the boys reported any formal engagement with education, training and/or employment immediately before their remands. Twelve (48 per cent) said that they had been permanently excluded from school, and a further nine (36 per cent) explained that they had not attended school. In most cases the boys' school exclusion/non-attendance had gone on for many years. None of the boys had any recognised educational qualifications.

- Seven (28 per cent) of the boys reported physical ill-health for which they were receiving treatment and seven (28 per cent) reported some history of mental ill-health.

- Almost half of the boys – 12 (48 per cent) – reported *regular* use of illicit drugs, and 17 (68 per cent) explained that at least some of their offending was directly attributable to alcohol misuse.

- Almost all of the boys – 23 (92 per cent) – reported regular occasions when they needed 'someone to talk to for advice, guidance and support'. However, 17 (68 per cent) explained that throughout their experience of growing up, they did not feel that there was any one person who they could turn to at such times.

Such backgrounds and challenging social circumstances are not uncommon for children in trouble, as noted earlier. Indeed, complex and layered patterns of disadvantage often characterise the social landscapes of child 'offenders', including family fracture; poverty; Social Services involvement; incomplete, unhappy and relatively unproductive school careers; unemployment; homelessness; isolation; and health-related problems frequently associated with alcohol and drug misuse (Goldson, 2000a). Such adverse conditions inevitably render children vulnerable, and prison remands can only serve to compound such vulnerability as is evident from the boys' comments below and throughout this chapter:

You should at least be allowed home. It hurts all the time. All you do is miss your family and you can't hack it sometimes. I wouldn't send kids to a place like this. I'd send them somewhere where they could go home at night. My Mum can't make it here to visit me. I wrote her letters but she doesn't write back. She has other kids to look after so I haven't seen her. It does my head in . . . It can crack you up inside. It hurts all the time. You shouldn't be away from your family – that's all there is to it. (Boy aged 16)

Sometimes the way the officers speak to you is bad. They don't seem to care about you. I don't want to get them in trouble but I'm just speaking the truth. (Boy aged 16)

I'm 15 and most of the time I'm locked in my cell 'cos there's no place in education for me and they've got nowhere else to put me.
(Boy aged 15)

There's a limit to what you can have in your cell. You can have more in your cell when you are sentenced. You can't have any posters. I can't even have a picture that my little sister drew for me.
(Boy aged 16)

It drags the time. I've got nothing to do but think when I'm on bang-up. No radio and I can't read. (Boy aged 16)

Not knowing when you are going to get out. You have nothing really to look forward to, no date to look forward to, nothing.
(Boy aged 16)

You see loads of little kids in here. There's one little kid who won't have a shower 'cos he's scared of being battered or shagged. He just won't have a shower. (Boy aged 16)

Horrible, its just horrible. That's all I can say. That's the only way I can explain it. (Boy aged 16)

FROM COURT TO PRISON

Nine (36 per cent) of the boys who were interviewed had previous experience of penal remand but the majority – 16 (64 per cent) – had never been remanded in prison before. Furthermore, 12 (48 per cent) said that they had not been advised to expect to be remanded when they appeared in court. This is consistent with far larger samples, and Her Majesty's Chief Inspector of Prisons (2000: 27) has noted that 'between a third and two thirds of unsentenced prisoners did not expect to be sent to prison and were unprepared for the experience'. Most of the boys described feelings of shock once they realised that they had been remanded to prison, and there was no discernible difference in the comments expressed by those with previous experience and a sense of expectation, and those without. Typical responses included:

The solicitor said it was 50/50 so I was hoping for the best. When they said it I felt really bad. When it sunk in I was scared. I didn't know what jail was like. I thought, 'I'm going to be taken away from my family.' I was worried that my Mum would be worrying about me. (Boy aged 16)

I was gutted. I felt I'd really messed up. I was just thinking all day, 'How have I got into this?' (Boy aged 16)

They said that I would be remanded to a secure unit but they had no beds so I had to come here. I was thinking that I couldn't cope. I was thinking about suicide. (Boy aged 15)

All escorting of juvenile remand prisoners from court to prison has now been privatised (*see* p. 78). Her Majesty's Chief Inspector of Prisons (1997: 28) has explained that the private escort contractors use 'cellular vehicles to transport young prisoners (and) each cubicle in these vehicles is about the size of a telephone box and contains nothing more than a bench seat and a small window'. Elsewhere, the Chief Inspector has noted that:

> . . . *recent inspections have given us cause for concern. Most [juveniles] travel long distances between court and the thirteen establishments across the country which hold them . . . At one establishment we spoke to juvenile prisoners who had experienced journeys of up to eleven hours, during which they claimed they were expected to relieve themselves in plastic bags as no comfort breaks were provided.*
>
> (Her Majesty's Chief Inspector of Prisons, 2000: 58)

The cubicles within the cellular vehicles are commonly known as 'sweatboxes', for obvious reasons. The boys who were interviewed were invited to describe their sweatbox journey from court to prison:

> *They handcuffed me like I was some animal and they made me feel stupid cuffing me like that. There was nothing I could do about it. They took me to the van and put me in a box. I felt very sad. Knowing that you are going to prison is not a good feeling.*
>
> (Boy aged 16)

> *It was a long journey, a very long journey. I was locked in a box the same size as that [pointing to a filing cabinet]. There is no toilet on the van. You can't have a piss, you have to wait. If you can't wait I suppose you just have to piss yourself.* (Boy aged 16)

> *I was thinking all sorts. I've got a kid and that, and I was thinking, 'I'm not going to see my kid and girlfriend.' I was just looking out of the window watching people walking and driving past, and I thought, 'I should be out there now.' I was thinking, 'What's it all going to be like? Will I get bullied?' I was shitting myself.* (Boy aged 15)

> *'The worse part was pulling out of Scunthorpe [the boy's home*

town]. It was horrible as I realised that I was getting miles and miles away from my family. I was shaking and scared. When the van got here I saw all the razor wire and stuff and I just wished that I could run away from it all. I was frightened, really frightened.

(Boy aged 15)

The initial shock that the boys describe experiencing in court is gradually replaced by the more detailed realisation of what awaits them. There is often a significant delay between the court's remand pronouncement and the child's arrival at prison, during which time they are either held in court cells while awaiting transit, or confined to the 'sweatbox' during it (*see* p. 82). Throughout this time the boys describe their mounting sense of fearful expectation, snowballing anxiety and dawning loss. By the time they arrive at the prison gates, their mental and physical well-being is likely to be at its most brittle and the need for sensitive reception and detailed assessment is self-evident. However, this is not to be.

PRISON RECEPTION AND VULNERABILITY ASSESSMENT

The complexities of risk assessment, and the inherent risks of flawed assessments are discussed in Chapter 3 (*see* pp. 63–64). The apparent shortfalls of the recently implemented vulnerability assessment processes for juvenile remand prisoners are considered in some detail in Chapter 4 (*see* pp. 92–94). The findings from the audit of ASSET and Post-Court Report documentation, which revealed significant information breakdown, has recently also been identified by Her Majesty's Chief Inspector of Prisons (2001a: 23): 'the present situation is not good, with too many young prisoners arriving at YOIs with virtually nothing known about them'. This dangerous situation was further confirmed, time and time again, during interviews with prison personnel and NRRI staff.

In interview, individuals from each group of staff were asked how often they received – and so had access to – the full-range of assessment documentation about child remand prisoners (i.e., the Remand Warrant, the Post-Court Report, the ASSET document and the Prisoner Escort Record – *see* pp. 74–78). Staff responses were recorded using a six-point scale ('all of the time', 'most of the time' (more than 70 per cent), 'more often than not' (50–69 per cent), 'in less than half of cases' (30–49 per cent), 'in less than one third of cases' (less than 29 per cent), 'rarely at all'). None of the 20 prison personnel interviewed chose either of the first two points on the scale.

Two (10 per cent) reported receiving all of the assessment documentation more often than not; six (30 per cent) in less than half of cases; five (25 per cent) in less than a third of cases, and seven (35 per cent) rarely at all. Of the 15 NRRI staff interviewed, none elected either of the first two points on the scale, like the prison personnel. The pattern of responses between the two groups of staff was similar, with two (15 per cent) of the NRRI interviewees electing the 'more often than not' option; three (20 per cent) the 'less than half of cases' option; four (27 per cent) the 'less than one third of cases' option, and the remaining six (40 per cent) the 'rarely at all' option.

In short, none of the staff interviewed from the participating Young Offender Institutions, or the NRRI, routinely has access to documentation – officially regarded as crucial for assessing the vulnerability of child remand prisoners. Sixty per cent of the Prison Service interviewees, and 67 per cent of the NRRI staff, could only report to receiving/having access to such information in less than a third of cases. Not surprisingly, neither group of staff was particularly satisfied with this.

The interviewees from each group of staff were asked whether they felt that the documentation at their disposal was adequate to inform assessments of children's vulnerability. Typical comments included:

If you receive it, it can be adequate, but most of the time you are working cold and its gut reaction on the basis of an interview, which can be very short, and probably not very accurate.

(Prison Officer)

If I get a completed, and completed well, ASSET, it gives very good pointers that I can follow further and expand upon. The PCR can also be very helpful if it is filled in well. The reality though is that I rarely have all of the necessary documentation. *(NRRI Practitioner)*

We very seldom get all of the information and we have to go on what the prisoner is telling us. We try to pick up on body language, eye contact and the like, but at the end of the day we just have to write down what they tell us. If they say 'no' to the history of self-harm question, for example, then I will simply write down 'inmate says no'. (Prison Officer)

When we don't get the information it's totally inadequate. Even when we do its not always adequate. There is real variation in standards: some are very good and some are diabolical in terms of the quality and detail of the information. We never seem to get the education information, which is very important in terms of vulnerability. If we give the inmates things to read, for example, then we have to be sure that they can read them. It's human bravado, they all say, 'Yeh I can read, boss' because it's weakness if they can't, but many of them can't. (Governor Grade Prison Officer)

Information, even when it is sent to the prison, does not necessarily reach the wing holding the kid. Recently, and all of a sudden, ASSETs, PCRs, everything disappeared from the wing files. The Governors decided that YOTs were blaming court staff, and court staff were blaming escorts, for any information that wasn't getting through. They realised that the prison would be held responsible if anything happened to the child, so they decided to chase for the information and then to store it all in one place, but the place is not the wing. To make matters worse the information is guarded very preciously and it is not always available, and this is by governor order. (NRRI Practitioner)

Prison personnel and NRRI staff are the frontline practitioners charged with the responsibility of assessing children's vulnerabilities at, or shortly after, their arrival at prison; and they simply do not have access to the basic information they need. The required documentation rarely arrives at the prison on time (if at all). On the few occasions when it does arrive, it is frequently incomplete, and it is not necessarily held in the part of the prison where it would be most useful. This raises concerns and casts serious doubt over the quality of assessments routinely carried out on vulnerable children.

Too often, prison personnel and NRRI staff have little more than 'gut reaction', instinct and the benefit of previous experience to draw on. The situation is made worse by an unsuitable physical environment, together with the crude, mechanistic, hurried and inexpertly executed nature of the reception assessment process itself.

The prison personnel were asked if there was adequate space and facilities (providing for privacy, confidentiality, lack of distraction and a comfortable interview) within the prison for the reception assessment of juvenile remand prisoners. Their responses were recorded using a four-point scale ('adequate', 'partially adequate', 'inadequate', 'don't know'). Only three (15 per cent) of interviewees chose the 'adequate' option; eight (40 per cent) chose the 'partially adequate' option; seven (35 per cent) the 'inadequate' option; and two (10 per cent) the 'don't know' option.

Similarly, the prison staff were asked if there was enough time at reception for the effective assessment of juvenile remand prisoners, and the same four-point scale was used to record their responses. Here none of the staff chose the 'adequate' option. Four (20 per cent) chose the 'partially adequate' option; 14 (70 per cent) the 'inadequate option'; and two (10 per cent) the 'don't know' option.

From the responses of the prison personnel, it would appear that the physical conditions within which vulnerability assessments take place are lacking, and the time available for such assessments is totally unsuited to the task. Explanatory comments included:

What we need is a private room. Too much is going on at reception. Sometimes at reception you just have to find a corner space, anywhere that is not being occupied. We used to be able to take them into a store cupboard but that's used for something else now.

(Prison Officer)

We have a private health care room, but we are very limited on space. It's a very small room, especially if we are doing a clinical procedure. (Senior Nurse)

It's usually busy and noisy and rushed at reception. It depends on the time that they arrive. There are times when kids are seen in court at half-ten in the morning and we get them at ten to seven

*at night. We then have to do reception, and everything that goes
with it, for up to 15 kids before half-eight.*

(Governor Grade Prison Officer)

*There is no room really. More often than not, if I'm honest, I don't
really interview them properly at all. They don't want to discuss
anything in front of anyone else. You just can't interview them at
reception. We receive them too late as well. We very rarely get
them before six o'clock and the shift system here just does not
allow for proper assessment. Even if you wanted to do your job
properly you're under real pressure from other staff who want to go
home. The whole roll of the jail has to be correct and in before
anyone can go. If I was still interviewing a new number [a recently
admitted child] the roll would not go in, which would mean that not
only every officer on the unit stays, but the whole jail stays. You are
trying to interview, but you know at the back of your mind that
everyone's waiting to go home so you rush it. (Prison Officer)*

The picture is clear. The reception, and so-called 'vulnerability
assessment' process, is like a cattle market. Children are herded into
crowded and unsuitable prison reception areas and processed with
indecent haste. The circumstances do not allow for anything else.
Despite the best individual efforts, late arrival, excessive numbers,
limited space and institutional imperatives produce inhumane
procedures. The range of experiences of such procedures is expressed
by the children themselves:

*You get rubbed down [searched], they take the details of the
offence, your name and all that. They take your clothes off you and
give you prison clothes. They ask if you are going to self-harm and
send you to a nurse. You just sit there and they ask if you are all right
and tick a box on this form. They ask if you are on medication and
tick a box. They just go through it like that until there's no more
questions. It doesn't take long. (Boy aged 16)*

*I heard the gates bang behind the van and I thought, 'That's it, I'm
banged up.' They booked me in and asked if it was my first time in
and I said, 'Yeh'. All they said was, 'Call me sir and all the women
officers miss.' They also said if you get bullied tell an officer. They*

*took the piss out of me a bit and then they sent me to a nurse
who asked if I was all right and I just said, 'Yeh'. I wasn't like, but
I couldn't explain to her how I felt. I felt that I would be unable to
cope . . . but I couldn't explain that to her. Then they just gave me
these clothes and a screw [prison officer] took me to my cell.*

(Boy aged 15)

*It's really scary – you don't know what to do and where to go. You
have a little interview with an officer and a nurse and they ask if you
know why you've been remanded, if you're all right, if you have any
health problems and if you're suicidal . . . I just said, 'I'm all right'
but I didn't know what to expect because I've never been in before.
I didn't really know if I was all right or not. I was just thinking, 'What
will it be like?', that's all I could think about. I wasn't really listening
to what they were telling me. I kind of wanted to get out of there
but I didn't want to go to my cell. It was weird. They just said that if
you ever get bullied or feel down, talk to an officer. I was thinking,
'Will they do owt? What if I do get bullied? If I told them, would it
stop?' You hear all these rumours about what happens to grasses
and I thought, 'There's no way I'm going to be a grass' but I was
really scared. (Boy aged 16)*

*I just felt really alone and down. They just spoke to me like I was
a piece of meat. They didn't make you feel like a person. I know
I broke the law and that, but they just treated me like a piece of shit.
They think 'cos you're in prison, and they're in uniform, they can just
tell you to do what they want and treat you as bad as they want.*

(Boy aged 16)

*I didn't know what was happening and when I asked questions they
just said, 'Shut up and speak when you're spoken to.' I didn't know
what was happening and what would happen next and all they did
was give orders, 'Sit there, stand there, go there.' They don't ask
anything accept name, number and what happened in court. Then
they strip searched me and I had to change into uniform. I felt
helpless. There's nothing you can do. I were frightened and I didn't
feel safe 'cos I was on my own. I didn't know no-one and I didn't
know nothing. I saw a nurse and they asked if I was on drugs.
I said, 'No' and she said, 'OK, you're all right.' (Boy aged 16)*

Her Majesty's Chief Inspector of Prisons (1997: 28) has explained that 'a positive start to his custodial experience is crucial for a young person, particularly a child. Reception is the area in which he first gains an impression of the establishment'. Despite both this, and the Chief Inspector's (2000: 119) subsequent emphasis on 'the importance of sensitive treatment in reception', the words from the children express anything but a 'positive start' and 'sensitive treatment'. There can be no doubt that some staff try harder than others, and this has also been observed by the most senior prison inspector: 'some reception staff seem to be aware that the process is intimidating and potentially dehumanising and adopt a suitably sensitive approach. Others seem not to understand this, to have become inured to it, or simply not to care' (Her Majesty's Chief Inspector of Prisons, 2000: 27). However committed the staff might be though, the conditions in which children are received at prisons preclude individual care. The pretence that a child's vulnerability can be accurately assessed in such hostile circumstances is deeply problematic. Furthermore, the notion that a child could be anything other than vulnerable at such a time is unreasonable. The child's 'first impression' is almost always one which intensifies trepidation, escalates fear and consolidates anxiety, and it is with such trepidation, fear and anxiety that the boy enters his cell for his first night inside.

FIRST NIGHT INSIDE

There is a developing volume of research which suggests that remand prisoners face a disproportionately high risk of self-harm and suicide, and that such risk is particularly acute on their first night and the early part of prison detention (*see* pp. 59–63). This applies, arguably even more so, to *child* remand prisoners. Indeed, Her Majesty's Chief Inspector of Prisons (1997: 30) has noted that:

> First night support is vital to children . . . new arrivals should be kept
> busy, and wing staff should ensure that verbal harassment of newly
> arrived children . . . is not tolerated. The immediate support that a

young prisoner receives on arrival in the wing should be provided by a designated member of staff and trusted young prisoners.

However, throughout the relatively lengthy course of research in the four Young Offender Institutions there was only minimal evidence of such 'first night support'. Indeed, some of the prison personnel had no hesitation in accepting this:

I don't think that we give them enough to stop thinking about themselves. We don't give them enough basic care. They need more one-to-one support but we just don't give it. We can't with the numbers of staff to kids. (Prison Officer)

It depends on what time they come in, whether or not they can be counselled. Most of them come in late so they're usually straight behind the door. (Senior Prison Officer)

There is no real first-night support. We might say that there is but it's all about back-covering really . . . If it says check every fifteen minutes and I do, I've done my bit, so it's not my fault if it [self-harm or suicide] does happen. That's hardly support though, is it?
(Prison Officer)

We have been very lucky here. We have only had one suicide and not that many attempted suicides. Bearing in mind the way that they are treated on the first night, this is more by luck than by design. (Prison Officer)

Within this context there was a striking irony in the pride that one interviewee expressed:

We are doing some good work around first-night support here. The first-night packs with radio, colouring book, crayons and comic is good practice. (Governor Grade Prison Officer)

Although colouring books, crayons and comics remind us that these remand prisoners are children – and raise uncomfortable questions about their confinement in prisons – they are unlikely to ease the profound discomfort of their first night inside. The children were asked if they had felt safe during their first night in prison. Only two (eight per cent) of the boys reported feeling 'safe' and neither provided reassuring explanations:

I'm used to being on my own so I felt all right, I suppose.

(Boy aged 16)

I felt safe because I was locked in and I knew that no-one could get to me. (Boy aged 16)

The overwhelming majority of children, however – 23 (92 per cent) – reported feeling 'unsafe':

I felt nothing really, just upset and sort of scared. I knew that I had to stop myself from being upset. I knew that I could not let anyone see me upset. (Boy aged 16)

I felt sorry for my Mum and sorry for the people that I burgled. I was scared because I'm not from this area and I wondered what the other lads would be like. As soon as I went in my pad I was thinking about what's going to happen to me tomorrow. (Boy aged 16)

I felt depressed a bit, a bit down like. I kept thinking, 'I should not be in here.' I wrote a letter to my parents to take my mind off it. I told them I was sorry and that I was all right, and I asked them if they would come and see me. (Boy aged 16)

I was crying, crying about my Mum and that. My Mum is being treated for cancer like I said, and I was worried about my little sister. She is only seven, and if my Mum dies she will grow up with no Mum. (Boy aged 16)

I was really scared in my pad. They are shouting at you through the windows and that, saying, 'I want your breakfast in the morning' and stuff like that. I was lying on my bed proper scared, thinking, 'I don't want to go out there in the morning, I don't want to go out at all.'

(Boy aged 15)

You don't know whose watching you, plus you've got your pad mate. You don't know who he is or what he is. Basically you just feel like there's lots of things running through your head. You can't sleep. You just think. You wonder, 'Am I going to get beat up?

Am I going to get killed?' There was loads of shouting out of the windows. I just didn't know what to do. I didn't even speak with my pad mate. I said nothing. I was too frightened. (Boy aged 16)

When you come in as a newcomer everyone comes to the windows and asks questions and takes the piss. I tried ignoring them at first but they don't stop, it goes on and on. I was very scared. You don't feel safe because you don't know nothing. You don't know what it's like. The main reason we are scared is getting bullied. You think prison is as rough as fuck and it makes you really scared.

(Boy aged 15)

The child's first night inside comes at the end of a bewildering day. Many will have started the day in police custody. All will have passed through court, and many will have been unprepared for its pronouncement. Most will have been held in court cells for several hours while awaiting 'sweatbox' transit to prison. Every child will have been processed at speed through prison reception, and many will have experienced the process as bedlam. The prison cell is the final destination where the distressing cocktail of fear, anxiety, regret, remorse, loss, loneliness and sleeplessness festers. The child's first-night thoughts are disturbed only by the shouting and banging of his fellow child-prisoners, which confirm the dread of bullying. The boy waits for the morning when his cell door opens and he enters the world of the prison wing.

ENDEMIC BULLYING

Bullying in all its forms – physical assault, sexual assault, verbal abuse, intimidation, extortion, and theft – is endemic within Young Offender Institutions. It is also very difficult to identify and combat. Each of the four participating Young Offender Institutions had official policies and anti-bullying strategies. Each displayed posters proclaiming that bullying would not be tolerated, and advising child prisoners what they could do should they be bullied. Many members of prison personnel expressed their antipathy to bullying in interview and affirmed the importance of such initiatives. However, despite all this, bullying remains a routine feature of prison life (*see* pp. 58–59).

Both prison personnel and NRRI staff recognised the entrenched nature of bullying. Each group of staff were asked how often bullying occurs and their responses were recorded using a five-point scale ('all of the time', 'most of the time', 'more often than not', 'not very often', 'not at all'). Of the 20 prison personnel interviewees, five (25 per cent) reported that bullying occurred 'all of the time'; four (20 per cent) 'most of the time'; eight (40 per cent) 'more often than not'; and three (15 per cent) 'not very often'. Of the 15 NRRI staff interviewed, five (33 per cent) chose the 'all of the time' option; eight (53 per cent) the 'most of the time' option and two (13 per cent) the 'more often than not' option. Although the prison personnel were apparently less inclined to believe that bullying might be happening all, or most of the time, there are important similarities between the responses of the two groups of staff. With the exception of three members of prison personnel, *all* the staff believe that bullying *at least* occurs 'more often than not', and despite any positive impact that they might have made, *none* of the staff believe that bullying has been eradicated by the various anti-bullying policies and practices that have been implemented. Typical explanations included:

It depends what you mean by bullying. I think that mental bullying, by which I mean eye contact, and body language, and verbal bullying, goes on all the time. You know it's there but there is no hard evidence, no bruises or cuts, just intimidation. The staff have clamped down on physical bullying, but the shouting through the windows is probably the worst. The kids are left to wait until the morning to see if the threats come true. The fear of that must be horrendous. (NRRI Practitioner)

We know it goes on . . . We do try and stamp on it and put a BIR [Bullying Incident Report] in on them, but things go on at night when we are not here. (Prison Officer)

The usual stuff about being small and wearing glasses, or if they look a bit different, or if their trainers are hanging off their feet.

It's amazing what they pick up on though. Also, if kids come from a different area they often don't want to come out from their cell. Just the noise means that kids don't want to come out and eat, and they will either do without and say they're not hungry, or they will eat in their cell. (Prison Officer)

Anybody can be a bully and anybody can be a victim, and they are not necessarily exclusive. Six-feet-five lads can be bullied by smaller lads if they have mates behind them. Many times you see lads and we think that 'victim' is written all over them, and pretty often they are. But sometimes they seem OK. It's difficult to tell. Very often, kids are being bullied by other kids who have just as many problems as the kid they are bullying. (Senior Prison Officer)

You have to have your staff switched on to it all the time. Even within the vulnerables you have a vulnerable who wants to be top. It's the nature of the beast – it's part of the prison itself.

(Senior Prison Officer)

We get an awful lot of boys who tell us but they can't tell the staff because the bullying is so severe, and they really believe that no-one can do anything. They are also very concerned about grassing and the fear that grasses get it even worse. (NRRI Practitioner)

I have said to young people, 'Have you not mentioned this to any of the officers?' and they say, 'There's none of the officers around her that I can talk to.' It's trust as well. If kids come into prison with all kinds of problems, they're not likely to trust us, are they?

(Staff Nurse)

It comes in waves, it depends who's on the wing. You get kids bullying each other, you get staff bullying kids and you get staff bullying staff. Some of us are deemed too soft. I talk to them as I talk to my own children. Other staff will say we're not strict enough in here because they're here for punishment, but we are not here to punish them further, are we? Outside the kids can get status in lots of ways. In here status is measured in different ways: fear and respect become very confused. Having lots of toiletries becomes status, so taking them off other kids takes place. They won't tell you

*because that's grassing and it's a sin to grass . . . It comes with
experience – seeing bullying, and then choosing how to deal with it.
You'll never get rid of it though, it's power, isn't it?* (Prison Officer)

The comments from prison personnel and NRRI staff paint a gloomy
picture of the permanent presence of bullying in all of its multifarious
forms; of prevailing 'dog-eat-dog' cultures in which the child can be
both victim and bully; and of the corrosive impact of bullying on
child remand prisoners. Bullying is, to borrow the words of the senior
prison officer above, the 'nature of the beast'. It is a 'beast' that
offers no relief and renders the bullied child powerless, for there is
nowhere for him to go. The compelling 'anti-grassing' ethic, coupled
with the self-defeating consequences of being labelled a 'grass',
effectively eliminates the prospect of help and protection. Moreover,
the fact that officer 'guardians' can also be bullies dispels any
lingering trust. None of this could be expressed more clearly than by
the children themselves:

*The officers try their best to stamp down on it, but it's because I'm
not from around here, I'm not from this area like, and I get it all the
time. There's the kids from Manchester who all stick together, and
there's the kids from Liverpool too. They say, 'It's a scousers' jail this
one', they think they run the jail. Then there's kids like me and we
get it from all of them.* (Boy aged 15)

*It happens every night at the windows – people shouting at each
other, and stress-heads banging on the pipes. Everyone running their
mouths off at the window and that. 'Window warriors' they call
them.* (Boy aged 16)

*The lad I am padded up with, his brother has just died, and they use
that against him at the window and that. It really upsets him, but
they just don't bother – they think it's just a laugh.* (Boy aged 15)

*A bigger lad gave me a crack, he said I was being cheeky. He was
seventeen I think, and I am fifteen, and I was thinking, 'How long is
this going to go on for?' There are fights all the time. Gym is where
it happens most often, somebody always gets picked on. It happens
walking back from education, anywhere where there's crowds.*

Some kids get told to order toiletries from canteen, and then they're taken off them. (Boy aged 15)

This lad gave me a half ounce of burn and said I had to pay him back a week later. I didn't know it was double back. He then wanted munch [crisps and biscuits] back too, and he kept on doubling it every week. He would shout through the window and threaten me and then everyone thought they can take me for a muppet [a vulnerable boy]. Every night they are shouting out the window, every single night, guaranteed. That's all you hear, that's all you hear every night. (Boy aged 16)

I am very lucky I suppose – my pad mate has been here for ages and he looks after me. He knows the tricks of the trade. I never go out of my cell much though . . . I've been out a couple of times on association, but I just feel much safer in my cell. This one lad in the next pad from me, the only time I get to see him is in education, but he gets bullied left, right and centre. He grassed up his pad mate for pinching his clothes, so he got beat up, and he gets bullied all the time. You can't grass anyone up. If you grass you get it all the time.
(Boy aged 16)

It's going on all the time – threatening you, shouting things, calling your mum names. There's nothing you can do about it. You just have to cope with it. I don't know how I do, you just do. My mate was hammered in the showers. When the screws asked him what was wrong he said that he fell over. If he had told him the truth, he'd have got hammered again. Most of the staff are all right but some either ignore you or try to wind you up. They swear at us and that, and call us names, and they threaten to drag us down to the block. Every day . . . bullying happens, there's a fight every day. It's getting worser and worser. A kid has just killed himself and I reckon that was through bullying. A sixteen-year-old lad . . . does not kill themself when they have their whole life in front of them. I just picture it in my head and it's bad, it's really bad. (Boy aged 15)

NO PLACE FOR CHILDREN

The prison personnel and the NRRI staff were invited to respond to the statement: 'It has been suggested that prisons are not appropriate for the purposes of holding juvenile remand prisoners.' Their responses were recorded using a four-point scale ('agree', 'partially agree', 'disagree', 'don't know'). Of the 20 prison personnel four (20 per cent) agreed with the statement, 11 (55 per cent) partially agreed and only five (25 per cent) disagreed. The 15 NRRI staff were – perhaps unsurprisingly – far more certain in their opinions, and 14 (93 per cent) agreed with the statement, with the remaining one (7 per cent) partially agreeing. Despite the different levels of emphasis and apparent certainty, however, it is noteworthy that all of the NRRI staff and 75 per cent of the prison personnel expressed doubts about the suitability of penal custody for remanded children. Indeed, a minority of the prison sample described their unequivocal commitment to disciplinary regimes as follows:

> I've been to a few secure homes and it's a complete waste of money. In general we get better behaviour from kids in prison. There is no discipline at the secure homes, no role model or father figure. When they come to this place it brings them to reality. It's the discipline side of it basically, they come here and hit a steep learning curve. We get them into line. They know what they can do, and what they can't do. (Senior Prison Officer)

Most, however, were far more circumspect. In this sense there was significant consensus between the prison personnel and NRRI staff, and a number of common themes emerged.

The first theme specifically related to untried children in prison. Both prison personnel and NRRI staff expressed concerns about this and typical comments included:

> They're not guilty of anything necessarily, it isn't an appropriate place for them, not at that age. (Prison Officer)

> Until they are sentenced and/or found guilty, they should not be in a prison environment, they should not be mixing with convicted people. The bail teams could do more. They sometimes think that

because this kid has been in trouble so many times, let's leave him to someone else. They give up on them. Everyone should be entitled to a service no matter what they are alleged to have done. It's beginning to seem as though you are guilty until proven innocent, rather than the other way around. (NRRI Practitioner)

The second theme emphasises the limitations of prison custody when measured against its own stated objectives to look after its young charges, to deter them (and others) from committing offences and to offer constructive rehabilitative interventions. Here both prison personnel and NRRI staff suggested that penal remands are at best ineffective, and at worse damaging:

We cannot guarantee their safety if we are honest. We fulfil a function for society, I suppose, in holding them until the courts decide what they want to do, but, in honesty, we do a very limited job. (Senior Prison Officer)

Prison is the last resort. With some there is no alternative. With others I look at them and think there is no way they should be in here, they need more one-to-one counselling and support. In secure accommodation you might have five staff to eight kids. Here you have four staff to sixty-five kids. As far as prisons go this place is not too bad, but prisons are not really any place for most of the kids we see on remand. (Prison Officer)

Prison doesn't work – it doesn't ensure the young people will come out of the system decent, law-abiding citizens. It creates anger and resentment, it makes low self-esteem worse, and it produces a lack of respect for anyone in authority. Many of these kids haven't even been found guilty. (NRRI Practitioner)

They are mixing with people who have been found guilty and they tend to learn and adopt inappropriate role models, but more than this, it is the trauma of coming into this environment and being locked behind a door. (Staff Nurse)

The third theme overlaps with the second, in emphasising the iatrogenic nature of penal remands, whereby the 'treatment' compounds the problems, placing not only the child at greater risk, but ultimately the general public too. Typical comments included:

I would say that looking around the prison as a snapshot on any day there is probably quite a lot of kids in here who could be dealt with better outside in the community. Are we the right people to look after these lads without any specialist training? I doubt it, because I think there is a real need for specialist training. We are expected to be parents, child psychologists, and nurses, all without training. I don't know what the alternative is, it's all down to cost and we are more cost effective than secure units, but it doesn't necessarily mean that this is the right place for them to be. Yes, they have committed crimes, but in all my experience I can tell you that prison is not a deterrent. We are just locking them up and keeping them off the streets for a few months, but they go straight back out to exactly the same situations that they have left. We had the perfect example today: a sixteen-year-old lad left here this morning with nowhere to live and no money. He'll soon be back in here. I don't think it does them any good to be in here – if anything, it changes them for the worse. (Senior Prison Officer)

I have had prisoners who I do not think should be in prison, but you have others, and the only way to stop them committing crime is to put them in custody, but I do not think that it does any good in the long run. I have had kids who you think just shouldn't be here: those who have done one-off crimes or others with mental health problems. For juveniles it just makes them worse people in the long run. (Prison Officer)

The fourth theme explicitly acknowledges that some children pose significant risks not only to themselves, but also to others. Both prison personnel and NRRI staff raised this in interviews. However, although they agreed that it might be necessary to restrict the child's liberty in such circumstances, they also acknowledged that prison generally remained an inappropriate means of doing this. The two prison officers quoted below captured this theme well:

It's a grey area. I can see the argument for both sides. Some of these lads need to be off the street, they are into heavy things, and need to be removed for public safety. But I also see the side that says it isn't doing them any good in here. We need to look at all these kids individually, but there's a massive amount of work to be done. There are many kids and I just think, 'There is no way they should be in here.' But there are others who should be right off the street. (Prison Officer)

I don't like the idea of locking kids up, and you are far more effective in working in the community. I also acknowledge though, that there are some kids who are dangerous and who need to be contained to reduce the risk both to themselves and to others. Some prisons can do that quite effectively. Others don't. If kids don't feel safe you increase all the problems. The regime that we are trying to develop here is an improvement, but it's far from ideal.

(Governor Grade Prison Officer)

The fifth theme introduced the difficult question of alternatives to penal remands and the perceived need to provide more imaginative, child-centred and effective responses. Typical comments included:

I think in the main they have been let down by the system altogether. They seem to get the bad end of everything and there is an attitude of blaming everything on young people, but offering them nothing. There are definitely cases where young people need controlling and accepting responsibility for their actions, but putting them in prison is no answer. It just becomes another part of their duff life – it is almost proof that all the agencies have failed. There is a desperate need for the agencies to be working more effectively to keep young people out of prisons and to keep the community safe.

(NRRI Practitioner)

I am not sure that we think hard enough about non-custodial options. We pander to the media, pander to the public, and don't take full account of non-custodial options. There is not a will to look at non-custodial options. I think we need to be really radical and start the whole process again. There has to be other options for these lads. There is some likelihood they may not get sentenced to custody at all, so why are we putting them through the whole trauma and drama of passing through the prison gates?

(Prison Chaplain)

In all, and despite some important differences in terms of certainty and emphasis as mentioned earlier, a general consensus emerged from the interviews with prison personnel and NRRI staff on the inappropriateness of prison for holding children on remand. Throughout the course of the interviews the children themselves also identified each of these themes. They also raise powerful and probing questions of justice. They also understand the ineffective nature of most custodial interventions. They, perhaps more than anyone, understand the corrosive and damaging impact of custodial regimes. However, despite their problems and irrespective of their pain, these children are generally not blind to the wider questions of criminal justice and community safety. Indeed, they also recognise that the public has a right to expect protection and, in satisfying that right, it is sometimes necessary to restrict the liberty of those whose actions threaten it. They also believe that alternatives must be sought for this purpose, because they also realise that prison is no place for children:

I reckon they should put us in a children's home or something.
I don't reckon they should put us in proper jails for adults. That is
what this place is, you know. We need more support, more people
who can talk to us and help us and that. I've had a bad enough life
and so have most of the kids in here. Some of us have done bad
things but I don't think it's right that we are locked up in here.
Bad things are done in here as well. What's the point in just doing
bad things to us 'cos we've done bad things? Some kids can't
handle it and can't cope. The ones that cope just get worse, like.
What good is that? (Boy aged 16)

Last night this kid, I don't know why, I think he was getting bullied
but I don't know. One of the officers opened this kid's door and he
just shouted, 'Get the nurse' and we were all put behind our doors.
No-one knew what was going on, but we all knew, if you see what
I mean. We heard them all rushing around and I reckon we all knew.
I knew. I thought about it all night, I couldn't stop thinking about it.
This morning when we came out for breakfast the screws said that
he had tried to kill himself and he was in hospital on a life support
machine. At dinner, they said he was dead. He was sixteen, the
same age as me. Everyone was very quiet. (Boy aged 16)

CHAPTER 7

Vulnerable children: beyond damaging systems

The aim of this concluding chapter is to draw together some of the principal themes of the book and to signal a direction for an alternative approach to vulnerable children. It provides an endnote that considers policy formation and practice development underpinned by rationality, social justice objectives and children's rights priorities.

CHILDREN AND VULNERABILITY

The complexities of defining and assessing children's vulnerability have been examined throughout the book. 'Vulnerability' is, in some respects, relative and can be moulded to suit policy imperatives, political exigencies, institutional capacity and different professional discourses. In other respects children's vulnerability is more 'real', located as it is within formidable material contexts (primarily poverty) and susceptible individual circumstances. In this latter sense Chapter 1 introduced the related concepts of *structural vulnerability* and *innate vulnerability*. The first relates to broad material realities and structural conditions, the second to the more narrowly defined specificities of individual circumstance.

The conditions that define structural vulnerability are rife in modern society. Despite the fact that the UK currently boasts the fourth strongest economy in the world, patterns of poverty and inequality have intensified over the last two decades, and such adverse conditions cut deep into the social fabric. In 1999/2000 14 million people – 25 per cent of the population – were living in poverty (below 50 per cent of mean income after housing costs) (Child Poverty Action Group, 2001). Within such *general* patterns the specific impact upon children is particularly problematic: '. . . children have been more vulnerable to poverty than society as a whole' (*ibid*: 39). Indeed, the disproportionate impact of poverty on children is clearly illustrated by the most up-to-date statistical evidence. For example, in 1979 ten per cent (1.4 million) of all children in the UK were living in poverty (using the same measure as above), but by 1999/2000 the corresponding figures had risen to 34 per cent or 4.3 million children (Department of Social Security, 2001).

The effects of poverty and inequality on children's lives are far-reaching: damaging their education, their health (mental and physical), their families, their housing, their neighbourhoods, their communities, their future prospects and their entire welfare (Goldson, Lavalette and McKechnie, 2002). Poverty and inequality permeate every crevice of the poor child's social landscape and, with depressing predictability, such injustice has a disproportionate effect on the lives of black children (Goldson and Chigwada-Bailey, 1999). These are the conditions that define structural vulnerability.

The same conditions invariably also damage inter-personal relations and family life. Children's opportunities and their experience of growing-up can be further stunted by family fracture, emotional neglect and even physical and sexual abuse. For children in such conditions, adults in general – and state agencies in particular – are often experienced as an unlistening, if not antagonistic, presence. It is at this precise juncture that structural vulnerability and innate vulnerability bond: it is on this point that the sights of child welfare and youth justice services are frequently, perhaps necessarily, focused. If it is not in secure and penal settings, it is within this damaging social space that the children who are the core concern of this book are normally to be found.

THE WELFARE AND JUSTICE CONSTITUENCIES: DIFFERENCES AND SIMILARITIES

It was noted in Chapters 1 and 2 that the vulnerabilities of children placed in secure accommodation under the provisions of civil/welfare law (the 'welfare constituency') are considered to be so great in the community, that restriction of liberty is sanctioned by the courts in order to keep them safe. In this sense their institutional confinement is conceived as a benign act. Conversely, in Chapters 1 and 3 the rationale for restricting the liberty of children by way of penal remands (the 'justice constituency') is seen to be quite different. Here, it is primarily the risk that children are thought to pose *to* the community, rather than the vulnerabilities that they might experience *within* it, that comes into play. Protection of the public takes precedence over protection of the child, and the restriction of liberty is essentially conceived in punitive/correctional terms.

There can be little doubt that some children place themselves and/or others at significant risk. Throughout the course of the research, I met children who had been 'rescued' from the most appalling, life-threatening circumstances, and I met others who were facing charges for very serious offences against the person. To a certain extent this 'endangered–dangerous' split confirms, even legitimises, the contrasting justifications for different institutions. However, to suppose that such institutions contain the *most* 'endangered' and 'dangerous' children in society is wrong. Even to assume that *every* child held in secure accommodation under civil/welfare statute is necessarily endangered, or that *all* children held on penal remands are inevitably dangerous, is misguided, as has been seen. The placement process is not a science and the apparent inconsistencies and injustices are such that it has been called a 'lottery'. Equally, to expect that children placed under civil/welfare statute in secure accommodation are qualitatively different to those held on penal remands under criminal/youth justice legislation is profoundly erroneous. There is significant interaction and overlap within and between the welfare-justice constituencies, and the backgrounds, social circumstances and experiences of such children are both complex and often similar.

As witnessed throughout this book, the similarities that such children share in their damaged backgrounds, their multiple vulnerabilities, and their manifest needs, are quite extraordinary. Furthermore, although they may be processed along different legal routes, their patterns of behaviour are often strikingly similar. Once such similarity is established, not only does the differentiation between the two constituencies become more opaque, but it is also far more difficult to fathom the starkly contrasting resources, conditions and treatment that characterise their respective institutional experiences. If such children have broadly similar needs, if their vulnerabilities overlap, if their behaviours and actions converge, then how can it be rational to place one constituency in compact Secure Units with intensive staff support, and the other on the anonymous landings of prison remand wings with minimal adult supervision and only the faintest shadow of care?

SYSTEMS BEHAVIOUR AND THE IMPACT OF POLICY

Irrespective of the similarities identified above and throughout this book, contemporary policy formation and practice development has accentuated the distinction between 'children in need' and 'young offenders' (Goldson, 2000a). On one hand, the Government has publicly set itself ambitious targets to end poverty, and restore social justice for children. A range of initiatives have been established, and substantial financial resources are being invested in new health, education and social care programmes. On the other hand, the policy emphasis on inclusivity and social justice for children is apparently conditional, and wider political imperatives have served to severely limit its application with regard to child 'offenders' (for a fuller discussion *see* Goldson, 1999; Muncie, 1999; Pitts, 2000). Policy is pitted with paradox in this respect.

Alongside the multitude of new initiatives to tackle child poverty, improve the range of children's services and promote inclusion and participation, the seemingly incongruent imperative to be tough on child crime has been grinding out a quite different range of policy and practice responses. Ultimately, the Government's 'no more excuses' agenda (Home Office, 1997) has produced a steady influx of younger and younger, and more and more, children into locked institutions, remanded and sentenced under criminal/youth justice legislation. A further paradox is apparent here. At precisely the same time that contemporary youth justice policies have produced unprecedented growth in the levels of child incarceration, developing concerns regarding the conditions and treatment of children in custodial institutions have been expressed from the most authoritative sources (*see*, for example, Her Majesty's Chief Inspector of Prisons, 1997 and 2001; Utting, 1997)

The apparent settlement with which the Government – through the Youth Justice Board for England and Wales – has sought to reconcile such paradox, is to be found in the reform of the juvenile secure estate. Prison Service Young Offender Institutions, Local Authority Secure Units and the privately managed Secure Training Centres have been drawn together within one estate. Such reform has primarily been directed towards children within the justice constituency but, as seen in Chapter 4, it has also made a very significant impact on the welfare constituency. Whatever its achievements, the very same reform is apparently facing insurmountable problems as a direct result of the policy paradoxes identified above. The extended powers that have been granted to the courts – in respect of secure/penal remands and custodial sentences – are taking their toll. Placement demand is significantly outstripping supply and such conspicuous imbalance is serving to undermine the more positive objectives of the reform effort. Manifestly vulnerable children continue to be placed within utterly unsuitable Prison Service institutions. The welfare constituency appears to be getting steadily squeezed out of the estate, and the staff at Local Authority Secure Units are having to revise their practice in ways that compromise the officially stated welfare ethos of secure accommodation. While the needs of the two constituencies of children are similar, the operational standards and increasingly 'offence focused' regimes, which are steadily being imposed upon Secure Units, are totally unsuited to those placed under the provisions of civil/welfare statute, and are arguably not particularly well-suited to the needs of the justice constituency either. Policy is far from joined-up and the system is behaving badly.

VULNERABILITY ASSESSMENT: RHETORIC AND REALITY

As noted earlier, defining vulnerability is complex, and assessing it is more complex still. By focusing upon the children who are held in secure and penal settings, this book has aimed to critically examine the instruments, methods and criteria that are used in order to assess their vulnerabilities. It has investigated the application and non-application of assessment processes including both the means by which, and the stage at which, a child's vulnerability is addressed/ assessed or not, as the case may be. It has explored the consistency of application both within each constituency of children and *between* the constituencies. The findings are not positive.

Although children who are placed in secure accommodation under the provisions of civil/welfare statute generally receive more detailed and expertly executed assessments than children in the youth justice system, both have significant shortcomings. For the welfare constituency, Chapters 2 and 5 provide detailed accounts of such imperfections, within which ineffective safeguards for the child are particularly conspicuous. Similarly, Chapters 3, 4 and 6 engage with the assessment methods that are applied to the justice constituency. Here, the complexities of assessment are given short shrift within a mechanistic, indecently hasty and deeply problematic process. Despite the rhetorical representations and associated claims made for each assessment process, the practical realities reveal serious defects in both.

INSTITUTIONAL RESPONSES: RELIEVING OR COMPOUNDING CHILDREN'S VULNERABILITIES?

Throughout this book it has been noted that there are a small but significant number of children who behave in such a way as to place their safety and/or the safety of others at serious risk. In these circumstances, restricting the liberty of such children is not, in itself, unreasonable. However, the children who are placed in secure and penal settings do not necessarily fall into the most endangered and dangerous categories. Putting this latter point to one side for a moment, it might be expected that secure and penal settings do succeed in effectively addressing the risks that children are judged to pose to themselves and others. Furthermore, it might be assumed that the positive effects of such institutional interventions endure the test of time. Despite the best efforts of the many people involved, however, there is little evidence of this on either the welfare or the justice fronts.

For secure accommodation and the welfare constituency, remarkably little is known of even the short-term 'outcomes' for children once they are discharged from secure settings, and even less is known about the medium- to longer-term effect. In Chapters 2 and 5 the immediate benefits of secure accommodation were considered by acknowledging that it facilitates temporary relief from the dangers of the street; it provides a comparatively safe enclosure; it offers some opportunities to attend to primary health needs and to re-build a sense of emotional well-being and self-worth, however fragile the foundations. The value of such tangible benefits should not be understated. Moreover, some of the staff who were interviewed presented a persuasive case that for certain children, interventions that serve to restrict liberty can also literally save lives. However, there is equally strong evidence to suggest that secure accommodation can be misused, and there is some evidence to suggest that it might even damage children. When it comes to evaluating the effectiveness of secure accommodation the messages are, at best, mixed on the basis of what little is known.

Turning to prison remands and the justice constituency, the evidence – which has been available for many years – is far less equivocal. On the basis of this substantial volume of evidence there can be no doubt that prison is not a suitable environment for children, and Chapters 3, 4 and 6 set out the detail of why this is so. There are, of course, people who rather stubbornly choose to argue that imprisoning children, however unsavoury, is ultimately the price that must be paid in order to stem the tide of child crime and protect the public from harm. However, the research evidence does not support this view. Indeed, locking up children is spectacularly ineffective in terms of preventing future offending. Children invariably leave prisons not only more damaged but also more angry, more alienated, more expert in the ways of crime and more likely to commit more serious offences (Goldson and Peters, 2000) – in fact more of everything that the children themselves, and the community at large, need much less of.

BEYOND DAMAGING SYSTEMS: RATIONALITY, SOCIAL JUSTICE AND CHILDREN'S RIGHTS

To lock up a vulnerable child is a sign of failure. To lock up the number of children that we do in England and Wales is failure in the extreme. It is not only ethically suspect but it is also irrational: it cuts across the grain of evidence derived in practice experience and research. In this respect, the practice of placing vulnerable children in secure and penal settings is markedly out of kilter with the prevailing drift of policy formation and practice development in the wider social care and criminal justice context. Elsewhere, approaches increasingly must be 'evidenced-based', interventions are of necessity driven by 'what works' priorities, 'best value' imperatives are pervasive, practice is routinely evaluated and 'outputs' are assiduously monitored.

More research is desperately needed to investigate the paths that lead some children towards damaging and dangerous patterns of behaviour. More longitudinal research is needed about effective interventions and the durability of such interventions. As argued elsewhere, however, such research will need to be carefully designed and must engage with the complexities faced by the children who are the subjects of intervention, the families and communities within which they grow up, and the professional agencies that work with them (Goldson, 2001a). Such research must also directly and actively consult with such groups, and the most determined efforts should be made to ensure that children as subjects are also afforded the fullest opportunities to participate and be heard. Although there is a pressing need for new knowledge, there is also a need for patience. New research evidence – good research evidence – can only emerge over time, and researchers, together with those who commission the research, must be bold enough, and honest enough, to say so.

However, such research will only be of value if it is rigorously applied to policy formation and practice development. To put it another way, policy and practice can only claim to be rational if it is rooted in reliable research evidence. There is no need to wait for the new knowledge in order to make a start: there is much to work with already. It is already *known* that locked institutions, and especially prisons, serve very little useful purpose for children. It is also *known* that the same institutions can be damaging, and that such damage is invariably long-lived – there is more than enough accumulated knowledge and evidence. Indeed, it is *known* that *fewer* such institutions are needed, not more – meaning *fewer* children in secure and penal settings. Knowing is not enough, however: this knowledge needs to be applied to resolute action. The tide of ever-increasing institutional growth must be reversed. Moreover, courage is needed to start a staged, but ambitious, closure programme.

The new direction for policy and practice development must be explicitly informed by social justice principles. Furthermore, such principles must apply equally to *all* children. Again there is no need to await the results of new research. It is no coincidence that the children who are placed within secure and penal settings are drawn from the most disadvantaged and damaged families, neighbourhoods and communities. This has been known for some time. The relation between structural vulnerability, innate vulnerability and problematic behaviour is not deterministic, but it is certainly correlative. Also, the behavioural dimension of this relation may be directed inwards or outwards, and it often takes both forms. Indeed, as seen earlier, the endangered–dangerous split is specious. It is no doubt nourished by competing professional interests, organisational and institutional convenience and/or political priorities, but its conceptual legitimacy is profoundly limited and flawed. There must be a move beyond a way of 'seeing' a child either as 'in need' and thus requiring care and protection, or as an 'offender' needing control and correction. Children within both the welfare *and* justice constituencies are first and foremost *vulnerable children* and they should be regarded and treated as such. Moreover, the conditions that create and sustain such vulnerability have to be systematically and comprehensively addressed. Treating symptoms, and invariably treating them badly in secure and penal settings, is simply not good enough.

Finally, and perhaps most importantly, the new direction for policy and practice must be underpinned by a totally unequivocal commitment to children's rights. Here too there is no need to wait. Many existing provisions of statute, together with international conventions, standards, treaties and rules, provide a strong foundation upon which to build (*see* Chapters 2 and 3). As a starting point in the quest for a more rational, more just, more effective and more dignified approach to troubled, sometimes troublesome – and always vulnerable – children, Article 3.1 and Article 37 (b) and (c) of the United Nations Convention on the Rights of the Child offer clarity:

In all actions concerning children, whether undertaken by public or private social welfare institutions, courts of law, administrative authorities or legislative bodies, the best interests of the child shall be the primary consideration.

No child shall be deprived of his or her liberty unlawfully or arbitrarily. The [restriction of liberty] . . . shall be used only as a measure of last resort and for the shortest appropriate period of time . . . Every child deprived of liberty shall be treated with humanity and respect for the inherent dignity of the human person, and in a manner which takes into account the needs of persons of his or her age.

Bibliography

ACOP and Nacro (1993) *Awaiting Trial.* London: Association of Chief Officers of Probation and Nacro.

Ashford, M. and Chard, A. (2000) *Defending Young People in the Criminal Justice System.* London: Legal Action Group.

Ashton, J. and Grindrod, M. (1999) 'Institutional troubleshooting: lessons for policy and practice'. In B. Goldson (ed.) *Youth Justice: Contemporary Policy and Practice.* pp. 170–90. Aldershot: Ashgate.

Audit Commission (1996) *Misspent Youth . . . Young People and Crime.* London: Audit Commission.

Aymer, C., Gittens, J., Hill, D., McLeod, I., Pitts, J., Rytovaata, M., Sturdivant, E., Wright, L. and Walker, M. (1991) 'The hard core – taking young people out of secure institutions'. pp. 92–112. In J. Dennington and J. Pitts (eds) *Developing Services for Young People in Crisis.* Harlow: Longman.

Backett, S. (1987) 'Suicide in Scottish prisons'. *British Journal of Psychiatry*, 151, pp. 218–21.

Bogue, J. and Power, K. (1995) 'Suicide in Scottish prisons 1976–1979'. *British Journal of Forensic Psychiatry*, 6, pp. 70–96.

British Medical Association (2001) *Prison Medicine: A Crisis Waiting to Break.* London: British Medical Association.

Bullock, R. and Little, M. (1991) *Secure accommodation for children.* Highlight no. 103. London: National Children's Bureau and Barnardos.

Cawson, P. and Martell, M. (1979) *Children Referred to Closed Units*. London: HMSO.

Chesney, D., Dickson, L., Fitzpatrick, J. and Uglow, S. (2000) *Criminal Justice and the Human Rights Act 1998*. Bristol: Jordans.

Child Poverty Action Group (2001) *Poverty: the Facts*. 4th Edition. London: CPAG.

Children's Legal Centre (1982) *Locked up in care: A Report on the Use of Secure Accommodation for Young People in Care*. London: The Children's Legal Centre.

Children's Legal Centre (2001) *Childright*. No. 175. Essex: The Children's Legal Centre.

Children's Rights Development Unit (1994) *UK Agenda for Children*. London: Children's Rights Development Unit.

The Children's Society (2001) *Annual Report from National Remand Review Initiative for the period 1st December 1999–30th November 2000*. London: The Children's Society.

Cohen, S. (1985) *Visions of Social Control*, Cambridge: Polity Press.

Corby, B., Doig, A. and Roberts, V. (2001) *Public Inquiries into Abuse of Children in Residential Care*. London: Jessica Kingsley Publishers.

Dawson, R. and Stephens, R. (1991) 'Applications for secure accommodation – a legal labyrinth'. *Justice of the Peace*, 155 (49), pp. 777–80.

Dennington, J. (1991) 'The mother of invention – negative reform and secure accommodation', pp. 74–91. In J. Dennington and J. Pitts (eds) *Developing Services for Young People in Crisis*. Harlow: Longman.

Department of Health (1990) *Children Act 1989 – Consultation Paper No. 1: Secure Accommodation (Guidance and Regulations)*. London: Department of Health.

Department of Health (1991) *Statutory Instrument 1505, Children and Young Persons. The Children (Secure Accommodation) Regulations*. London: Department of Health.

Department of Health (1993) *The Children Act 1989 Guidance and*

Regulations: Volume 4: Residential Care. Third impression. London: HMSO.

Department of Health (2000) *Framework for the Assessment of Children in Need and their Families.* London: The Stationery Office.

Department of Health (2001) *Children Accommodated in Secure Units, year ending 31 March 2001: England and Wales. Statistical Bulletin 2001/17.* London: Department of Health.

Department of Social Security (2001) *Households Below Average Income.* London: Department of Social Security.

Donovan, P. (2002) 'Long term rise in prison custody for young people breaks past pledges'. *Community Care,* 10–16 January, p. 16.

Dooley, E. (1990) 'Prison suicide in England and Wales 1972–1987'. *British Journal of Psychiatry,* 156, pp. 40–45.

Elkins, M., Gray, C. and Rogers, K. (2001) *Prison Population Brief England and Wales: June 2001.* London: Home Office.

Farrant, F. (2001) *Troubled Inside: Responding to the Mental Health Needs of Children and Young People in Prison.* London: Prison Reform Trust.

Gabbidon, P. and Goldson, B. (1997) *Securing Best Practice.* London: National Children's Bureau.

Gabbidon, P. and Goldson, B. (1998) *Preparing to Care.* London: National Children's Bureau.

Goldson, B. (unpublished, 1992) *'Incarcerative Child-Care': A Critical Analysis of Secure Accommodation.* MA Thesis. Lancaster: University of Lancaster.

Goldson, B. (1995) *A Sense of Security.* London: National Children's Bureau.

Goldson, B. (1997) 'Children in trouble: state responses to juvenile crime'. In P. Scraton (ed.) *'Childhood' in 'Crisis'?*, pp. 124–45. London: UCL Press.

Goldson, B. (1997a) 'Children, crime, policy and practice: neither welfare nor justice'. *Children and Society,* 11, pp. 77–88.

Goldson, B. (1999) 'Youth (in)justice: contemporary developments in policy and practice'. In B. Goldson (ed.) *Youth Justice: Contemporary Policy and Practice*, pp. 1–27. Aldershot: Ashgate.

Goldson, B. (1999a) *Black Youth, Crime and Criminalisation: Justice System or Systemic Injustice?* Commissioned paper submitted to the Runnymede Trust Commission on the Future of Multi-Ethnic Britain, see *The Parekh Report (2000) The Future of Multi-Ethnic Britain*. London: Profile Books.

Goldson, B. (ed.) (1999b) *Youth Justice: Contemporary Policy and Practice*. Aldershot: Ashgate.

Goldson, B. (ed.) (2000) *The New Youth Justice*. Lyme Regis: Russell House Publishing.

Goldson, B. (2000a) "Children in need' or 'young offenders'? Hardening ideology, organisational change and new challenges for social work with children in trouble'. *Child and Family Social Work*, 5, (3), pp. 225–65.

Goldson, B. (2001) 'Behind locked doors: youth custody in crisis?'. In *Childright*, 173, pp. 18–19. Essex: The Children's Legal Centre.

Goldson, B. (2001a) 'A rational youth justice? Some critical reflections on the research, policy and practice relation'. *Probation Journal*, 48, (2), pp. 76–85.

Goldson, B. (2002) 'New punitiveness: the politics of child incarceration', pp. 386–400. In J. Muncie, G. Hughes and E. McLaughlin, (eds) *Youth Justice: Critical Readings*. London: Sage.

Goldson, B. and Chigwada-Bailey, R. (1999) '(What) justice for black children and young people?', pp. 51–74. In B. Goldson (ed.) *Youth Justice: Contemporary Policy and Practice*. Aldershot: Ashgate.

Goldson, B., Lavalette, M. and McKechnie, J. (eds) (2002) *Children, Welfare and the State*. London: Sage.

Goldson, B. and Peters, E. (2000) *Tough Justice: responding to children in trouble*. London: The Children's Society.

Goldson, B. and Peters, E. (unpublished, 2002) *National Remand Review Initiative: Final Evaluation Report (December 1, 1999–November 30, 2001)*. Prepared for the Youth Justice Board for England and Wales.

Goldson, B., Peters, E. and Simkins, L. (unpublished, 2001) *National Remand Review Initiative: Interim Report (December 1999–November 2000)*. Prepared for the Youth Justice Board for England and Wales.

Harris, R. and Timms, N. (1993) *Secure Accommodation in Child Care: Between Hospital or Prison or Thereabouts?* London: Routledge.

Hatty, E. and Walker, J. R. (1986) *A National Study of Deaths in Australian Prisons*. Australian Institute of Criminology: Canberra.

Hendrick, H. (1994) *Child Welfare: England 1872–1989*. London: Routledge.

Her Majesty's Chief Inspector of Prisons (1996) *Patient or Prisoner? A New Strategy for Healthcare in Prisons*. London: Home Office.

Her Majesty's Chief Inspector of Prisons (1997) *Young Prisoners: Thematic Review by HM Chief Inspector of Prisons for England and Wales*. London: Home Office.

Her Majesty's Chief Inspector of Prisons (1999) *Suicide is Everyone's Concern: A Thematic Review by HM Chief Inspector of Prisons for England and Wales*. London: Home Office.

Her Majesty's Chief Inspector of Prisons (2000) *Unjust Deserts: a Thematic Review by HM Chief Inspector of Prisons of the Treatment and Conditions for Unsentenced Prisoners in England and Wales*. London: Her Majesty's Inspectorate of Prisons for England and Wales.

Her Majesty's Chief Inspector of Prisons (2001) *Report of Her Majesty's Chief Inspector of Prisons December 1999–November 2000*. London: Home Office.

Her Majesty's Chief Inspector of Prisons (2001a) 'Reflections of a Chief Inspector'. *Youth Justice*, 1, (1), pp. 17–27.

Hodgkin, R. (1995) *Safe to Let Out? The Current and Future Use of Secure Accommodation for Children and Young People*. London: National Children's Bureau.

Home Office (1984) *Suicide in Prisons: Report by Her Majesty's Chief Inspector of Prisons*. London: HMSO.

Home Office (1997) *No More Excuses – a New Approach to Tackling Youth Crime in England and Wales*. The Stationery Office: London.

Home Office Circular 30/1992, Local Authority Circular LAC (92)5, Welsh Office Circular 21/92 (1992) *Criminal Justice Act 1991: Young People and the Youth Court*. London: Home Office and Department of Health, and Cardiff: Welsh Office.

Home Office (1998) *Speaking Up for Justice*. London: Home Office.

Home Office (2001) *Persistent juvenile offenders – courts to get new powers*. Home Office Press release, 27 February. London: Home Office.

Howard League (1995) *Banged up, Beaten up, Cutting up: Report of the Howard League Commission of Inquiry into Violence in Penal Institutions for Teenagers under 18*. London: The Howard League for Penal Reform.

Howard League (1997) *The Howard League Troubleshooter Project*. London: The Howard League for Penal Reform.

Howard League (1999) *Desperate Measures: Prison Suicides and their Prevention*. London: The Howard League for Penal Reform.

Howard League (2001) *Children in Prison: Provision and Practice at Castington*. London: The Howard League for Penal Reform.

Howard League (2001a) *Children in Prison: Provision and Practice at Lancaster Farms*. London: The Howard League for Penal Reform.

Hughes, R. and Thompson, B. (2000) 'Under 18 year olds: making the difference'. *Prison Service Journal*, 128, pp. 4–7.

Inquest (2000) *Death of Teenager in Feltham Young Offender Institution*. Press release. prewww.gn.apc.org/inquest/press/hensonpr. html.

Inquest (2001) *Statistical Information: Deaths in Prison (England and Wales)*. www.gn.apc.org/inquest/prisonstats.html.

Kerfoot, M. (2000) 'Youth suicide and deliberate self-harm'. In P. Aggleton, J. Hurry and I. Warwick (eds) *Young People and Mental Health*, pp. 111–27. Chichester: Wiley.

Lader, D., Singleton, N. and Meltzer, H. (2000) *Psychiatric Morbidity among Young Offenders in England and Wales*. London: Office for National Statistics.

Leech, M. and Cheney, D. (2001) *The Prisons Handbook*. Winchester: Waterside Press.

Levenson, J. (2000) *A Hard Act to Follow? Prisons and the Human Rights Act*. London: Prison Reform Trust.

Liebling, A. (1996) 'Prison suicides: what progress research?' In A. Liebling (ed.) *Deaths in Custody: Caring for People at Risk*, pp. 41–53. London: Whiting and Birch.

Liebling, A. (1999) 'Doing research in prison: breaking the silence?' *Theoretical Criminology*, 3, (2), pp. 147–73.

Liebling, A. and Krarup, H. (1993) *Suicide Attempts and Self-Injury in Male Prisons*. London: Home Office.

Lyon, J., Dennison, C. and Wilson, A. (2000) *'Tell Them So They Listen': Messages from Young People in Custody*. London: Home Office.

Macpherson, Sir W. (1999) *The Stephen Lawrence Inquiry: Report of an Inquiry by Sir William Macpherson of Cluny*. Cmnd 4262-1. London: Stationery Office.

Malek, M. (1993) *Passing the Buck: Institutional Responses to Controlling Children with Difficult Behaviour*. London: The Children's Society.

McCausland, J. (2000) *Guarding Children's Interests: The Contribution of Guardians ad litem in Court Proceedings*. London: The Children's Society.

McFarlane, A. (2001) 'Law notes'. *Representing Children*, 13 (4), pp. 273–77.

McHugh, M. and Snow, L. (2000) 'Suicide prevention: policy and practice'. In G. Towl, L. Snow and M. McHugh (eds) *Suicide in Prisons*, pp. 1–25. Leicester: British Psychological Society.

Medlicott, D. (2001) *Surviving the Prison Place: Narratives of Suicidal Prisoners*. Aldershot: Ashgate.

Mental Health Foundation (1999) *Bright Futures: Promoting Young People's Mental Health.* London: Salzburg-Wittenburg.

Millham, S., Bullock, R. and Hosie, K. (1978) *Locking Up Children: Secure Provision within the Child Care System.* Farnborough: Saxon House.

Moore, S. and Smith, R. (2001) *The Pre-Trial Guide: Working with Young People from Arrest to Trial.* London: The Children's Society.

Muncie, J. (1999) *Youth and Crime: A Critical Introduction.* London: Sage.

Nacro (1988) Juveniles Remanded in Custody, *Nacro Briefing*, November. London: Nacro.

Nacro (1991) Juveniles Remanded in Custody, *Nacro Briefing*, September. London: Nacro.

Nacro (1994) *Young Offenders Committee Policy Paper 3 – Rethinking Remands for Alleged Young Offenders Remanded in Custody.* London: Nacro.

Nacro (1998) Bail Support, *Nacro Briefing*, September. London: Nacro.

Nacro (1999) Court Ordered Secure Remands, *Nacro Briefing*, May. London: Nacro.

Nacro Cymru (2000) *Custodial remands amongst young people in Wales during 1997/98.* Swansea: Nacro Cymru.

Nacro Cymru (2000a) 'Secure Accommodation in Wales'. *Youth Crime Wales: the quarterly journal on youth crime in Wales*, 2, Editorial.

Neal, D. (1996) Prison suicides: what progress policy and practice? In A. Liebling (ed.) *Deaths in Custody: Caring for People at Risk*, pp. 54–67. London: Whiting and Birch.

Newbronner, E. (2002) 'Taking a Count of Vulnerable Children'. *Community Care*, 24–30 January, pp. 40–41.

Newburn, T. (1995) *Crime and Criminal Justice Policy.* London: Longman.

Novick, L.M. and Remmlinger, E. (1978) 'A Study of 128 Deaths in New York City Correctional Facilities (1971–1976)'. *Medical Care*, 16, pp. 749–56.

O'Neill, T. (1999) 'Locking up Children in Secure Accommodation: a Guardian *ad litem* Perspective'. *Representing Children*, 11, (4) pp. 289–97.

O'Neill, T. (2001) *Children in Secure Accommodation: a Gendered Exploration of Locked Institutional Care for Children in Trouble.* London: Jessica Kingsley Publishers.

O'Neill, T. (unpublished, 2001a) Secure Accommodation for Children in Trouble: Care or Custody? Paper presented at the Nineteenth Annual Conference of the Howard League for Penal Reform – *Villains and Victims: Children and the Penal System*, New College, Oxford, September 2001.

Penal Affairs Consortium (1996) *Juveniles on Remand: Recent Trends in the Remanding of Juveniles to Prison Service Custody.* London: Penal Affairs Consortium.

Pitts, J. (2000) 'The new youth justice and the politics of electoral anxiety'. In B. Goldson (ed.) *The New Youth Justice*, pp. 1–13. Lyme Regis: Russell House Publishing.

Pitts, J. (2001) *The New Politics of Youth Crime: Discipline or Solidarity.* Basingstoke: Palgrave.

Roberts, M. (2001) 'Youth justice news'. *Youth Justice*, 1, (1), pp. 56–62.

Sinclair, I. and Gibbs, I. (1998) *Children's Homes: A Study in Diversity.* Chichester: John Wiley.

Smith, D. (1999) 'Social work with young people in trouble: memory and prospect', pp. 148–69. In B. Goldson (ed.) *Youth Justice: Contemporary Policy and Practice.* Aldershot: Ashgate.

Stein, M., Rees, G. and Frost, N. (1994) *Running the Risk.* London: The Children's Society.

Stern, V. (1998) *A Sin Against the Future: Imprisonment in the World.* London: Penguin.

Timms, J. (1995) *Children's Representation: A Practitioner's Guide*. London: Sweet and Maxwell.

Towl, G. and Crighton, D. (2000) 'Risk assessment and management'. In G. Towl, L. Snow and M. McHugh (eds) *Suicide in Prisons*, pp. 66–92. Leicester: British Psychological Society.

Towler, K. (1999) 'Bail or jail?' *Safer Society*, 2, pp. 20–21. London: Nacro.

Travis, A. (2002) 'Courts to lock up child robbers'. *The Guardian*, 16 April.

United Nations General Assembly (1989) *The United Nations Convention on the Rights of the Child*. New York: United Nations.

Utting, Sir W. (1997) *People Like Us: The Report of the Review of the Safeguards for Children Living Away from Home*. London: HMSO.

Vernon, J. (1995) *En Route to Secure Accommodation*. London: National Children's Bureau.

Wade, J., Biehal, N., Clayden, J. and Stein, M. (1998) *Going Missing: Young People Absent from Care*. Chichester: John Wiley.

Warner, N. (2001) *Sentencing Juveniles to Custody*. Circular mailed to all youth Courts and Youth Offending Teams in England and Wales, 20 August. London: Youth Justice Board for England and Wales.

Woolf, Lord Justice (1991) *Prison Disturbances April 1990: Report of an Inquiry by the Rt Honourable Lord Justice Woolf and His Honour Judge Stephen Tumin*. London: Home Office.

Worrall, A. (1999) 'Troubled or troublesome? Justice for girls and young women', pp. 28–50. In B. Goldson (ed.) *Youth Justice: Contemporary Policy and Practice*. Aldershot: Ashgate.

Youth Justice Board (1998) *Juvenile Secure Estate: Preliminary Advice from the Youth Justice Board for England and Wales to the Home Secretary*. London: Youth Justice Board for England and Wales.

Youth Justice Board (2000) *National Standards for Youth Justice*. London: Youth Justice Board for England and Wales.

Youth Justice Board (2000a) *Review of the Year 1999–2000*. London: Youth Justice Board for England and Wales.

Youth Justice Board (2000b) *ASSET Bail Assessment Profile*. London: Youth Justice Board for England and Wales.

Youth Justice Board (2000c) *Post Court Report*. London: Youth Justice Board for England and Wales.

Youth Justice Board (2001) *Reform of the Juvenile Secure Estate – a four year plan by the Youth Justice Board*. London: Youth Justice Board for England and Wales.

Youth Justice Board (2001a) *Delivering Change: Youth Justice Board Review 2000/2001*. London: Youth Justice Board for England and Wales.

Youth Justice Board (2001b) *Youth Justice Board News*, Issue 8. London: Youth Justice Board for England and Wales.

Youth Justice Board (2001c) *T1:V – Initial Custodial Reception Assessment – Guidance for Completion*. London: Youth Justice Board for England and Wales.

THE CHILDREN'S SOCIETY
A POSITIVE FORCE FOR CHANGE

The Children's Society is one of Britain's leading charities for children and young people. Founded in 1881 as a Christian organisation, The Children's Society reaches out unconditionally to children and young people regardless of race, culture or creed.

Over 100 projects throuhout England
We work with over 40,000 children of all ages, focusing on those whose circumstances have made them particularly vulnerable. We aim to help to stop the spiral into isolation, anger and lost hope faced by so many young people.

We constantly look for effective, new ways of making a real difference
We measure local impact and demonstrate through successful practice that major issues can be tackled and better resolved. The Children's Society has an established track record of taking effective action: both in changing public perceptions about difficult issues such as child prostitution, and in influencing national policy and practice to give young people a better chance at life.

The Children's Society is committed to overcoming injustice wherever we find it
We are currently working towards national solutions to social isolation, lack of education and the long-term problems they cause, through focused work in several areas:
- involving children in the regeneration of poorer communities
- preventing exclusions from primary and secondary schools
- providing a safety net for young people who run away from home and care
- seeking viable alternatives to the damaging effects of prison for young offenders.

The Children's Society will continue to raise public awareness of difficult issues to promote a fairer society for the most vulnerable children. For further information about the work of The Children's Society or to obtain a publications catalogue, please contact:
The Children's Society, Publishing Department, Edward Rudolf House, Margery Street, London WC1X 0JL. Tel. 0207 841.4400. Fax 0207 841 4500.
Website: www.childrenssociety.org.uk
The Children's Society is a registered charity: Charity Registration No. 221124.